Beyond the Lens

Rights, Ethics & Business Practice in Professional Photography

Published by

The Association of Photographers Ltd

with the support of

The Design & Artists Copyright Society

Kodak

PROFESSIONAL & PRINTING IMAGING

BTEC

Business & Technology Education Council

Dedicated to the memory of Vic Goodman

First edition 1994, edited by Jill L. Anthony
Second Edition 1996, edited by Jackie Kelley
Reprinted January 2000

Published by The Association of Photographers Limited
Registered Office: 81 Leonard Street, London EC2A 4QS.
Tel 020 7739 6669 Fax 020 7739 8707 E-mail aop@dircon.co.uk Web www.aophoto.co.uk
Printed by Ashford Press, Southampton

ISBN 0 9523517 5 7

Introduction

It is my great pleasure to welcome you to this second edition of Beyond the Lens, The Association of Photographers' reference book on current photographic business practice.

We created Beyond the Lens as an extension of our ongoing commitment to raising professional standards for all within our industry; be they student, commissioner or practitioner. It is our belief that the process of business is a collaborative effort - nowhere more clearly seen than in the creative industry. With this in mind, we have created a unique consolidated volume, which distills our 25 years of service to the photographic community and blends that with vital input from the other quarters of our "neighbourhood".

Thanks to this, you will find Beyond the Lens is a comprehensive overview of the ethics, standards and expectations that our clients have of us. We have, therefore, drawn particular emphasis to areas which we know continue to be sources of friction, such as copyright for example. You will find practical guidelines to assist you through your dealings in these areas; members of The Association will, of course, be able to seek day to day advice from our offices as necessary. Please remember, that these chapters reflect not only our thoughts, but also the recognised working practices of advertising agencies, design groups and editorial commissioners.

When The Association of Photographers successfully campaigned for photographers to have the ability to control their work through the Copyright Designs and Patents Act 1988, photographers acquired new rights. For those of us already in business, this necessitated a major change in the way we negotiated with clients; to those who inherit these automatic rights, we realise our duty of education in their sanctity. To this end, The Association is passionately committed to the educational process of younger photographers. We maintain close links with most UK colleges, and continue to support and guide students as they complete their studies and, ultimately, become our assistants and fellow professional photographers.

Photographers must always strive to achieve parity when appropriate, and lead where necessary; not just in business, but artistically. We trust that Beyond the Lens creates a framework which frees photographers to create valuable new work within a solid ethical context.

Finally, we must take this opportunity to thank Kodak for their continued support of this project, and for providing all members with a complimentary copy. That Kodak recognises the symbiotic nature of our business relationships, proves the spirit I believe you'll find expressed in Beyond the Lens.

Michael Harding
Chairman
The Association of Photographers

About the Publisher

The Association of Photographers is a non-profit making association. It was first launched in 1968 as The Association of Fashion and Advertising Photographers, and a few years later expanded to include editorial photographers. Our principal aims have remained the same: to promote the highest standards of work and practice throughout the industry, and to protect and improve the rights of all professional photographers in the UK. The Association has its own gallery and annual awards shemes, which showcase its members' work. Other publications produced by The Association include Image magazine and various awards books.

About the Authors

For the writing of Beyond the Lens, The Association of Photographers called upon many experts within the photographic industry and related business services:

Janet Ibbotson joined the Design & Artists Copyright Society in 1992 as Deputy Chief Executive and is responsible for DACS' work as the representative collecting society for visual artists in the UK (including photographers). She previously worked as General Secretary of The Association of Photographers (1985-1992), and, as Secretary of the British Photographers Liaison Committee (then the Committee on Photographic Copyright), she was closely involved in lobbying for changes in the law, which resulted in the 1988 Copyright Designs and Patents Act.

Gwen Thomas has worked for The Association of Photographers since 1987 and is currently Company Secretary, Deputy Chief Executive and Rights Advisory Manager, dealing with legal, ethical and copyright problems. She sits on the British Copyright Council, IPA Arts Buyers committee and is Secretary for the British Photographers' Liaison Committee and Pyramide UK - liaising with the European Pyramide and the European Parliament - and is a member of the British Literary and Artistic Copyright Association.

Jill L. Anthony worked for The Association of Photographers from 1989-1995 as the Manager for Resource and Professional Development. She worked closely with colleges and advised on photographic education and careers and as well as representing the Association as a Director of the Photography and Photo-Processing Industry Training Organisation. Jill was the editor of the first edition of Beyond the Lens.

Paul Rochman is a qualified accountant with his own accounting company - Rochman Goodmans, Chartered Accountants.

John Godden is a financial adviser with Blacktower Capital Limited, independent financial advisers.

John Williamson of Williamson Carson Insurance Brokers has many years of experience within the photographic industry.

Other contributors to this edition are: Martin Beckett, professional photographer and Honorary Managing Director of Pyramide Europe; Jonathan Trapman, professional photographer; Sal Shuel, former Secretary of the British Association of Picture Libraries & Agencies; Susan Griggs, photographers' agent; and Paul Hobgen, The Association of Photographers' Financial Adviser.

Acknowledgements

Thanks to everyone who has contributed to this, the second edition of Beyond the Lens.

To the authors: Janet Ibbotson, Gwen Thomas, Jill L. Anthony, Paul Rochman, John Godden, Martin Beckett, Paul Hobgen, John Williamson, Jonathan Trapman, Sal Shuel and Susan Griggs; and to the late Vic Goodman for his help with the first edition.

To Neal Davies of Kodak and Janet Ryeland of the Business & Technology Education Council for their support of both the first and second editions.

To Charles Swan of the Simkins Partnership for casting his legal eye over the final draft.

To all the volunteer readers who studied the drafts, especially: David A. Bailey, Terry Beddis, Richard Clark, Peter Dazeley, Carol Fox, Mark Gaskin, Michael Harding, Michelle Kenny, Carl Lyttle, Alan Marsh, Sandra Molloy, Janice Nemitz, and Stuart Wheeler.

And to Gwen Thomas, Anna Bailey, Emma Fox, Mary Drew and Valerie May for providing welcome backup and support.

Jackie Kelley
Editor

Contents

This book contains twelve Units with clearly defined Elements. Cross referencing is included in the text for further reading in the book. These references appear as three numbers in brackets, which refer to the Unit number, the Element number and the page, eg. (u2:e5:p30) refers to Unit 2, Element 5, page 30. The text also makes reference to forms and documents reproduced at the back of the book. References to illustrations are shown in italics and include the illustration and page numbers, eg. (*ill 3:p109*) refers to Illustration 3, page 109.

Introduction 3

About the Publisher 3

About the Authors 4

Acknowledgements 4

Unit 1 UK Copyright Law 11

INTRODUCTION 11

ELEMENTS

1 **What is Copyright?** 11
- A Human Right
- The Common Law Tradition v. Droit d'Auteur
- Intellectual Property
- Which Copyright Act?
- A Usage Right - Mainly a Reproduction Right

2 **Key Points of the Copyright, Designs & Patents Act 1988** 12
- a) Protected Works
- b) Artistic Works
- c) Definition of a Photograph
- d) Authorship
- e) Ownership
- f) Employed Photographers
- g) Duration of Copyright

3 **Identifying and Protecting Photographic Material** 16

4 **Licensing the Use of Photographs** 16
- Assignment or Licence?
- More reasons not to assign copyright
- The main terms of the Licence
- Exclusive Licence

5 **The Commissioned Photographer and Copyright** 19
- Advertising Photographers
- Editorial Photographers
- Taking the Long Term View

6 **The Non-Commissioned/Library Photographer** 20

7 **Copyright and The Student** 20

8 **Fair Dealing and other Permitted Acts** 21
- News Reporting and Current Events
- Criticism and Review
- Research and Private Study
- Educational Use
- Libraries and Archives
- Off-Air Recording of Television Programmes
- Reprographic Copying - Photocopying and Slice Collections
- Incidental Inclusion
- Advertising the Sale of a Photographic Work

9 **Rights in Underlying Works** 23
- Collage

CONTENTS

Copyright in Photographs of Other Protected Works
Certain Artistic Works on Public Display
The Publisher's Right
10 Infringement of Copyright and Remedies 24
SUMMARY 25

Unit 2 Moral Rights 27

INTRODUCTION 27
ELEMENTS
1 What are Moral Rights? 27
2 Key Points 27
a) The right to be identified as the author or director, known as the 'Paternity Right'
b) The right to object to derogatory treatment of a work - known as the 'Integrity Right'
c) The right not to have a work falsely attributed to a person as its author or director - known as the False Attribution Right
d) The right to privacy in respect of certain photographs and films - known as the Privacy Right
3 Duration of Moral Rights 29
4 Consent and Waiver of Moral Rights 29
5 Moral Rights in Practice 30
6 Breach of Moral Rights 30
7 Philosophy of Moral Rights 31
SUMMARY 31

Unit 3 Standards & Codes of Practice 33

INTRODUCTION 33
ELEMENTS
1 Portfolio Presentation 33
2 Fees 33
3 Pre-Production/Experimental & Speculative Photography 33
4 Bookings/Art Orders 34
5 Expenses and Advances 34
Model fees
Film and Processing charges
Insurance
Labour/Subcontractors
Studio & equipment
Props
Transport and travel
6 Cancellation and Postponement 35
7 Rejection and Non-use of Work 36
Rejection
Rejection after the shoot
Rejection of work on technical grounds
Non usage of accepted work
8 Liability of Work/Materials 36
9 Paperwork 36
a) Estimate
b) Invoice
c) Licence
d) Model Release Form
e) Delivery Note
10 Payment 38
11 Freelance Assistants 38

Assisting Photographers
Bookings
Cancellation and Postponement
Fees and Payment
Location Work
SUMMARY 40

Unit 4 Ethics (Principles of Best Practice) 41

INTRODUCTION 41
ELEMENTS
1 **Privacy** 41
Use of People in Advertisements
Defamation
Model Release Forms
Possible Privacy Legislation
2 **Trespass** 42
Taking Photographs in a Public Place
Permits
3 **Trade Marks, Stamps and Money** 43
4 **Confidentiality** 43
Advertising Photography
Editorial Photography
5 **Passing Off** 44
Photography
Photographic Assistants
6 **Plagiarism** 45
7 **Photographer and Client Relationship** 45
8 **Photographer and Supplier** 45
Loss and Damage of Film
Goods in Trust
9 **Photographer, Agent and Library** 46
Picture Libraries
Agents
SUMMARY 47

Unit 5 Contracts and Licensing 49

INTRODUCTION 49
ELEMENTS
1 **Basic Contract Law** 49
2 **Photographer and Client** 49
3 **Client and Photographer** 49
4 **Equitable Assignments** 50
5 **Third Parties** 50
6 **Terms and Conditions** 51
7 **Legality and Retrospective Orders** 52
8 **Negotiating Licences** 52
Advertising
Editorial
SUMMARY 55

Unit 6 Europe 57

INTRODUCTION 57
ELEMENTS
1 **What Harmonisation means for Photographers** 57
What is the European Union?

What is Harmonisation?
How do Photographers have a say in Harmonisation?
Pyramide
Key Areas of Policy which affect Photographers
2 **Copyright** 59
3 **Working Practice** 59
4 **Working in other parts of Europe** 60
SUMMARY 60

Unit 7 Tax and National Insurance 61

INTRODUCTION 61
ELEMENTS
1 **Income Tax: Self-Employment and Employment** 61
2 **Self-Employment - Notifying the Inland Revenue** 61
3 **Accounts and Bookkeeping** 62
Simple Tax Accounts - for Earnings up to £15,000
Operating Account
Balance Sheet
Depreciation/Capital Allowances
4 **Contacting the DSS Contributions Agency** 65
National Insurance Classes
National Insurance Number
5 **Self Employment - Class 1 NI Contributions on Schedule D Earnings** 66
6 **Self-Employment - Class 2 and Class 4 NI Contributions** 67
Class 2 NI Contributions
Exception Certificate from Class 2 NI Contributions
Class 4 NI Contributions
7 **Self Assessment and the Current Year Basis of Accounting** 68
8 **Budget 1995** 69
SUMMARY 69

Unit 8 Value Added Tax (VAT) and Customs & Excise 71

INTRODUCTION 71
ELEMENTS
1 **What is Value Added Tax** 71
2 **Registration for VAT** 72
Eligibility
Compulsory Notification
Voluntary Registration
Advantages of being VAT Registered
Disadvantages of being VAT Registered
VAT Invoices - Invoicing clients for VAT amounts
How to Register for VAT
3 **VAT and Trading Abroad/Export of Photography** 73
4 **Accounting and Record Keeping** 73
SUMMARY 74

Unit 9 Insurance & Liabilities 75

INTRODUCTION 75
ELEMENTS
1 **Optional Insurance Policies** 75
Personal Accident Insurance
Income Protection Insurance
Loss of Business/Business Interruption
Critical Illness

Motor Insurance Additional Premiums
Weather Contingency
Equipment Insurance
Film Insurance
Portfolio Insurance
Goods in Trust
Policy Excesses
2 **Public Liability Insurance** 79
3 **Employer's Liability Insurance** 79
Photographic Assistants and Public & Employer's Liability
4 **Professional Indemnity Insurance** 80
Professional Indemnity Cover
Exclusions
5 **Working Abroad** 81
Employer's Liability
Public Liability
SUMMARY 81

Unit 10 Collecting Societies 83

INTRODUCTION 83
ELEMENTS
1 **Brief Background to Collecting Societies** 83
2 **What is a Collecting Society?** 83
3 **Secondary Rights** 84
4 **How Collecting Societies Licence** 84
5 **Design and Artists Copyright Society (DACS)** 85

Unit 11 Advanced Business 87

INTRODUCTION 87
ELEMENTS
1 **Sole Traders; Partnership; Limited Company** 87
Sole Traders
Partnerships
Limited Companies
2 **Bookkeeping** 88
3 **Credit Control** 88
4 **Opening Accounts with Suppliers** 89
5 **Borrowing Money** 89
Business Plans
6 **Factoring** 90
7 **Prizes and Awards** 90
8 **Leasing and Asset Finance** 90
Hire Purchase
Lease Purchase
Contract Hire or Leasing
9 **Pensions, Savings, Investments and Mortgages** 91
Pensions
Savings & Investment
Income Replacement
Financial Advice
Commercial Lending
Residential Mortgages
10 **Claiming Benefit** 95
What help is available?
How long does it take?
Mortgage Relief

Exemptions from Social Security Benefits
What to expect when signing on

Unit 12 Digital & Electronic Imaging 97

INTRODUCTION 97
ELEMENTS
1 The Impact of the New Technologies 97
2 What use are the New Technologies? 97
a) The Tool
b) The Medium or Carrier
c) Creative Form
3 What Rules? 98
The Importance of the Reproduction Right
Copyright in Photographic Works in Digital Form
Digital Rights
4 How to Licence Digital Use 100
The Licence for Digital Use
5 Moral Rights in the Digital Environment 101
6 Other Digital Issues 102
Copyright in the Digital Version of a Photograph
Appropriation of other Artistic Works
Copyright in Underlying Works
Confidentiality and Privacy
7 Protecting Photographs on the Internet 103

Illustrations

1 Standard Estimate Form 105
2 Standard Invoice Form 107
3 Licence to Use 109
4 Assisting Photographer's Invoice 111
5 Delivery Note 113
6 Model Release 115
7 Base Usage Rate Guidelines 117
8 Agent/Photographer Agreement 121
9 BAPLA Photographer/Picture Library Contract 123
10 P45 Part 1 - Inland Revenue: Statement of Tax & Earnings 125
11 CWF 1 - Notification of Self-Employment 127
12 CA72B - Contributions Agency: Deferment of Class 4 NI Contributions 129
13 CF10 - Contributions Agency: Application for Class 2 Exception Certificate 131
14 VAT 1 - Customs & Excise: Registration Form 133
15 VAT 100 - Customs & Excise: VAT Return Form 137
16 Example Bank Receipts Record Sheet 139
17 Example Bank Payments Record Sheet 141
18 Example Petty Cash Record Sheet 143
19 Example Invoice Record Sheet 145

Appendix

Permits 147
Useful Addresses 148
Useful Forms, Pamphlets & Publications 149

Index 151

Unit 1 : UK Copyright Law

INTRODUCTION

A knowledge of copyright law and its application, and an understanding of how to combine copyright law with contract law, are essential for the success of any photographer. Copyright and contract law are key components in the successful negotiation of rights, usage and fees, and thus are central to the photographer's earning ability, irrespective of the type of photography carried out. Copyright, like creativity, should be an integral part of every photographer's working life. This unit details the principles of copyright law and explains how this law has an impact on the professional dealings of the photographer.

ELEMENT 1 : WHAT IS COPYRIGHT?

A Human Right

Article 27 of the Universal Declaration of Human Rights states that:
1) Everyone has the right to freely participate in the culture of the community, to enjoy the arts and to share in scientific advancement and its benefits.
2) Everyone has the right to the protection of the moral and material interests resulting from any scientific, literary or artistic production of which they are the author.

This combination of the need for public access to the products of the human intellect, with protection for the rights of the creator of those products, enables them to continue creating, and has resulted in the development of the system of copyright.

The Common Law Tradition v. Droit d'Auteur

The Common Law Tradition, as developed in the UK and the USA, emphasises the economic exploitation and dissemination of creative works, making the rights in those works into pieces of property. The Droit d'Auteur principle behind most European legislation, is more of a human right and places the personal or moral rights (see Unit 2) of the creator before commercial interests. In the Droit d'Auteur tradition, the economic rights arise from the moral rights. In the Common Law Tradition economic rights come first.

Intellectual Property

Copyright is one of a wider group of rights called 'intellectual property' rights. 'Intellectual' because they are products of the human mind and 'property' because they are owned like a house or other form of property.

It is essential to note that, although such rights attach to 'products of the human mind', the rights only come into existence once the work is 'fixed' in the form of a painting, cast as a bronze, or 'fixed' on a negative or transparency. No rights exist in an idea, but only attach to the physical manifestation of that idea, that is the painting, manuscript, photograph or sculpture.

Intellectual property in the UK covers patents, trade marks, designs and, of course, works protected by copyright. Copyright legislation in the UK also covers Moral Rights (see Unit 2).

Which Copyright Act?

In the UK, copyright works are protected under the Copyright Designs and Patents Act 1988, which became effective on the 1st August 1989, but in some instances the 1956 Act or 1911 Act will still apply to certain works. Guidance on their application is to be found in the 1988 Act.

Since the 1988 Act was introduced, there have been a number of revisions to the Act. These result from the overlapping effect of other areas of UK legislation (eg. Acts covering Broadcasting), or from the implementation of European Legislation intended to harmonise intellectual property law across Europe (eg. the Commission's Directive on the Duration of Copyright). Implementation of Directives from the European Union are generally in the form of a Statutory Instrument. For photographers the most important and relevant amendments to the 1988 Act have been in the adoption of the Statutory Instrument on Duration (u1:e2g:p14).

A Usage Right - Mainly a Reproduction Right

Copyright is the right of the creator to reproduce or copy their own work and to authorise others to reproduce or copy that work. This right is granted exclusively to the creator of the work and gives them control of their work. Thus, for the creator, copyright is a sword and a shield; a sword with which to carve a living, and a shield to protect their work from misuse or abuse.

There are other categories of rights which apply, for example, those which relate to the broadcasting and distribution of copies of works, and, in the future, legislation may provide new rights for certain types of digital use; but for the photographer it is the reproduction right which is of greatest importance.

ELEMENT 2 : KEY POINTS OF THE COPYRIGHT, DESIGNS AND PATENTS ACT 1988 (referred to as the 1988 Act)

a) Protected Works

Protection under the 1988 Act is afforded to the creators of original literary, dramatic, musical or artistic works.

Note the use of the word 'original'. Nowhere in the 1988 Act is the term 'original' defined and there have been very few legal cases which have established the basis of originality. For the purposes of copyright protection, most photographs in the UK are treated as original. This is not the case in all European countries.

b) Artistic Works

Included in this category of protected works are paintings, graphic designs, sculptures, illustrations, works of artistic craftsmanship and, of course, photographs.

c) Definition of a Photograph

The definition in the 1988 Act reads as follows:
"'photograph' means a recording of light or other radiation on any medium on which an image is produced or from which an image may by any means be produced, and which is not part of a film".

This definition covers photographs in all their forms, and holograms, but does not include a still taken from a 'film', that is from a movie or video or broadcast programme. The definition of films and the rules which apply to them are quite separate.

d) Authorship

The creator of a protected work is known as the 'author'. This term does not just apply to writers, but covers the creator of every protected work, and has a legal meaning of its own. In the case of a photograph, the author is 'the person who creates it' and that, normally, is the photographer, not the assistant who loads the film and perhaps presses the button on the camera, nor the art director who provided the rough and the initial concept, nor the stylist who dressed the set, but the photographer.

Photographers have not always been recognised as the authors of their photographs and these old rules continue to cause a good deal of confusion. Under the 1911 and 1956 Act the commissioner - whether a person or a company - owned the copyright of the photograph they had commissioned. To make matters worse, 'the author' was the person who owned the film at the time the photograph was taken. Thankfully none of this applies any longer; photographers are however frequently approached by clients who think one variation or another still applies.

Example : Client's position: "I've paid for you to take the photograph so I own it and any copyright in it."

The response of the photographer should be: "You are paying me for my skill and creativity; you are paying for my time and the expenses of the photographic shoot; you are paying for the right to use the photograph in your advertisement or editorial; but you do not own the copyright and ultimately you cannot own the photographic image. You must return it to me when the agreed period of use is complete. The photograph is my copyright and I am the person best placed to preserve and protect my work."

e) Ownership

1. The Link between Authorship and Ownership

The law states that the author of a work is the first owner of any copyright in that work. As explained in the previous section, the author of a photograph is the photographer. Hence the photographer is the first owner of copyright in every photographic work he/she creates.

2. Ownership of Materials and Ownership of Copyright

The ownership of copyright in artistic works, including photographs, is quite separate from the ownership of the actual physical work.

Example A painter sells a painting for a sum of money, to be hung on a collector's wall. The collector does not acquire the copyright for that payment, only the right to hang it on the wall and perhaps at some stage in the future to resell the painting. The copyright remains with the painter and it is up to that painter to exploit the right should they wish.

Although the material object and the copyright can be quite separate, most photographers, illustrators and graphic designers, working commercially, will find it easier if they ensure they retain some claim to the ownership of the physical material. For instance, it is standard practice for illustrators to have the original artwork returned to them when the licence period is finished, if not before. For cartoonists, if a client wishes to keep the artwork they normally pay a separate sum to purchase the artwork and hang it on their wall, even if they have already paid for the materials as part of the commissioning fee.

For photographers, particularly where there are many out-takes from a shoot, keeping control of the originals is vital.

3. Works of Joint Authorship

It is possible for a single work to have two or more authors and thus two or more copyright owners; however, this is not generally recommended because of the obvious complications of controlling and permitting use of the work. Joint authors should not just rely on the future goodwill of their creative partner, but should have an agreement in writing from the very beginning, perhaps a section in a wider partnership agreement which covers all aspects of the business relationship. Leaving joint copyright matters to fate and the vagaries of friendship is unwise and could ultimately be very expensive.

4. Assignment of Copyright

The photographer may choose to transfer the ownership of copyright in a particular photograph to someone else, through an assignment of copyright. The law states that such an assignment must be made in writing and signed by the photographer, but in some cases other forms of agreement, including a verbal agreement, can have the same effect (u5:e4:p50).

In nearly every situation it should be unnecessary for the photographer to assign copyright. The best way for a photographer to permit the use of their work is by issuing a licence. A licence permits use without transferring ownership of the copyright (u1:e4:p16).

5. Partial Assignment of Copyright

It is possible to partially assign copyright. On the face of it, this may seem attractive when dealing with a client who wishes to fully acquire certain rights in the photographs. It is not recommended because of the complications involved in controlling the use of the material and in deciding who should hold the original photographs.

When assigned, copyright lasts for exactly the same period as it would normally, ie. life of the photographer plus 70 years. Sometimes clients ask for an assignment of copyright for a specified period of time, on the basis that copyright will be reassigned after that time. This is possible, but the client's requirements can quite easily be satisfied by the inclusion of specific clauses in the contract and licence for use, and an assignment is not necessary.

f) Employed Photographers

Employed photographers do not hold the copyright of any work produced 'in the course of their employment', instead copyright is owned by the Employer.

In UK law, generally there is very little clear guidance as to what constitutes an employed person; however, it is generally taken to be someone who works under a contract of employment (or contract of service), whose tax and National Insurance contributions are deducted before receipt, and whose employee contributions are paid by their employer (u7:e1:p61). Where possible, employed photographers should ask their employers to insert a clause into their employment contract which states that the photographer owns the copyright and not their employer, but of course it is very difficult for those seeking employment or accepting a position to insist on or even ask for such a clause to be included in their employment contract.

A freelance photographer who accepts a commission from a client which lasts for a short period of time, eg. a photography residency, should ensure that they are issued with a contract for services and not an employment contract or contract of service. Even better, as a responsible freelancer, the photographer should issue their own contract.

One final point to note, employed photographers should be careful of how and when they take photographs outside the hours of their employment. For example, if an employed photographer uses their employer's equipment, film, darkroom and business contacts, or takes their own pictures at the end of a shoot for their employer, then it is possible that in a court of law these factors could contribute to a decision that the copyright lies with the employer.

g) Duration of Copyright

Copyright in a photograph lasts for the life of the photographer plus 70 years. When the 1988 Act was first introduced this was not the case, but on the 1st January 1996, Statutory Instrument No. 3297 introduced regulations which increased the duration of copyright in the UK in line with a European Union Directive which applies to all member states of the European Economic Area (EEA), and the introduction of these regulations has resulted in amendments to the 1988 Act. A further Statutory Instrument, introducing additional further regulations which are of major importance for photographers, should be in force by the end of 1996. The first set of regulations (SI3297) relate to:

- new works created on or after January 1st 1996;
- existing works.

To understand the regulations, it is important to know the meaning of two key terms. These are 'extended copyright' and 'revived copyright'.

The provisions for extended copyright apply to works protected by copyright under the 1988 Act immediately before January 1996. These are works which were still in copyright at the end of 1995 under the life plus 50 years rule.

The provisions for revived copyright apply where the term of protection had previously expired in the UK before December 31st 1995, but where the works were protected by copyright in any EEA State on July 1st 1995.

General points worth noting are that the regulations legislate on ownership of both revived and extended copyright. They cover existing licences, agreements and waivers or assertions of moral rights, and use of revived works, introducing a compulsory licence for the use of these works. This compulsory licence means that, with certain exceptions, the work may be used without the permission of the copyright owner if the owner is given sufficient notice and a reasonable fee is paid. Nothing in the regulations affects pre-existing moral rights (u2:e2:p27).

The regulations are intended to apply to photographs in exactly the same way as they do to other artistic works, that is for the life of the author plus 70 years (except where the term of protection is longer under the 1988 Act), thus increasing the term of protection by 20 years.

It would be confusing and largely irrelevant to devote much space to the general details. Those interested in finding out more about the general effect of the regulations should contact the Design & Artists Copyright Society (DACS) for a copy of their

Information Booklet (the following section on the regulations in relation to photography are reproduced with the permission of DACS), or the British Photographers Liaison Committee (BPLC) who may be able to advise on suitable publications (see Appendix, page 148).

Much of the work of interpreting these regulations will come, in time, from the experience of those working in the field and also from legal decisions, but the main changes are outlined below.

Photographs made on or after January 1st 1996
These will be automatically protected for the life of the author (the photographer - being the creator of the work) plus 70 years.

Photographs made after August 1st 1989, but before or on December 31st 1995
These would have been first protected under the 1988 Act for the lifetime of the photographer plus a period of 50 years from the end of the year in which he or she died. They now attract life plus 70 years.

Photographs made on or after June 1st 1957 but before August 1989
These would have first been protected under the 1956 Copyright Act for a period of 50 years from the end of the year in which the photograph was first published.

If the photograph is unpublished as at August 1st 1989, the period of copyright protection is for a specific period of 50 years from the end of 1989, that is to 31st December 2039. Do remember, though, that the new regulations specify that if the term of protection under the 1988 Act is longer than that determined by the regulations, then the longer term will prevail, eg. previously unpublished or anonymous photographs.

The period of copyright protection is now to be calculated on the basis of the author's life plus a period of 70 years - the publication date is no longer a relevant factor. For the purposes of calculating the duration of copyright protection, the author is interpreted to mean the photographer. However, the 1956 definition of author may still cause problems in relation to the ownership of copyright.

Photographs made before June 1st 1957
Photographs made during this time were originally protected under the 1911 Act for a period of 50 years from the end of the calendar year in which they were taken (regardless of whether they were published or not).

The author under the 1911 Act was the person who owned the negative - not necessarily the photographer or even a human person. Again, the new period of copyright protection will apply to photographs taken at this time by reference to the author defined in the 1988 Act - so for these purposes the photographer will be the author. So in respect of photographs made during or after 1945, the rules of Extended Copyright will apply.

In respect of photographs made before 1945, where copyright in the UK would have expired before December 31st 1995, but where at July 1st 1995 such photographs were still in copyright in one member state in the EEA, the copyright will be revived for the remainder of the period of the author's life plus 70 years (see below).

It should be noted that 'films' made before June 1st 1957 were not protected as 'films' or cinematographic works, but as dramatic works and as a series of photographs.

Ownership of Revived Copyright in Photographs
The owner of any revived copyright is the person who owned the copyright immediately before it expired. The owner is referred to in the Regulations as the 'former copyright owner'.

If the former copyright owner died before January 1st 1996, or if the former copyright owner was a company which before that date ceased to exist, the owner of the revived copyright will be the author's heirs or beneficiaries.

Example A publishing company commissioned and published a photograph taken by a photographer in 1940. The publishing company owns the copyright as a result of the commission. The publishing company also owns the original negative, and did so at the time at which the photograph was taken. Copyright in the photographs, under the 1911 Act, lasts for a period of 50 years from the end of the year in which the photograph was taken, therefore copyright in the UK expired at the end of 1990. However, say this photograph was protected in France on July 1st 1995. The publishing company is unfortunately no longer in existence, but the copyright in the photograph is now revived for a period of 70 years from the end of the year in which the 'author' died (being the photographer in accordance with the new definition). However, as the publishing company no longer exists, there is no former copyright owner, so ownership of the revived copyright should vest in the 'author' or the heirs.

ELEMENT 3 : IDENTIFYING AND PROTECTING PHOTOGRAPHIC MATERIAL

Photographers should ensure that all work, whether transparency or print, is identified as follows:

© A. Photographer, 1996
Moral Rights Asserted
This work may not be reproduced without the permission of
A. Photographer, Address, Tel No.

This information should appear somewhere on the photograph (normally on its reverse) every time it is sent out. It should also accompany films and should be incorporated in some way into every piece of paperwork issued by the photographer, for example on delivery notes.

Photographs sent to clients or potential clients should always be accompanied by a delivery note (u3:e9e:p38, *ill 5:p113*) which lists the works enclosed, states that the photograph must not be reproduced without permission and must always be credited to the photographer. Supplying work on a speculative basis can be risky, but if the photographer feels it is the only way to attract the attention of potential editorial clients, then every photograph should be accompanied by appropriate paperwork and statements of copyright.

The paperwork involved in recording and marking photographs may seem tedious now, but establishing good practice at an early stage when there are relatively few photographs to record and even fewer being reproduced, will prepare the photographer and their emerging collection for the future. A properly archived collection is more accessible, and has more useful information attached for the researcher to use, than a pile of negatives, transparencies and prints thrown into a cupboard and stored in less than ideal conditions when their immediate usefulness is past.

ELEMENT 4 : LICENSING THE USE OF PHOTOGRAPHS.

By assigning copyright in a photograph, the photographer renounces all control over their work (although they are still able to exercise their moral rights), and they are no longer in a position to earn from that photograph. For the photographer it is not a recommended way to do business. A much more satisfactory alternative is to grant a licence to the user (u5:e8:p52, *ill 3:p109*).

For photographers, the decision to assign copyright or not has become a major issue, because clients, sometimes through ignorance, sometimes through avarice, and only very occasionally through need, insist on an assignment of copyright. Such an assignment will often appear as part of the contractual terms which are issued to the photographer before the job is done. These terms are to be found on the paperwork received from the client, often in the small print on the reverse of the client's written order form.

Assignment or Licence?

It is essential to know the difference between an assignment of copyright and a licence which permits the use of the photograph. Perhaps the easiest way to learn about the difference is to draw parallels between copyright which, as already explained, is a 'property' right, and other property rights which are more readily understood, such as the ownership of a freehold house.

	House	Copyright
1.	A person occupies the whole of their house.	The photographer holds copyright and no-one else is granted the right to use the photographs.
2.	A person rents or leases the whole house to another individual.	The photographer licences someone to reproduce their work in any media, in any territory or for any time period.
3.	A person rents out a room or a flat to another individual.	The photographer grants a publisher the right to publish in a single edition of a consumer magazine within the European Community. *or* The photographer licences an advertising agency to run a 48 sheet poster campaign on 90 sites in the UK and Australia over a two year period.
4.	A person sells the freehold of their house.	The photographer assigns the copyright in their work.

Once these principles have been understood, then licensing becomes much easier.

Looking at the options available in the above list, it is far better in the long term, and whenever it is possible, to take the third of these options, that is to give the client a limited licence. The photographer should, of course, negotiate with their client on the basis of whichever option gives the best deal (u1:e4c:p18).

If, for whatever reason, the photographer uses option 4, and assigns their copyright as they would sell a freehold property, then they should recognise they will have no further interest in, or control over, their work (other than through moral rights) and there may be no further opportunity for the photographer to earn from that photograph. Someone else can do with it as they will. If an assignment of copyright is absolutely necessary, then the photographer must make sure it's worth while - after all, no-one sells their house for the price of a week's rent!

More Reasons not to Assign Copyright

It cannot be emphasised strongly enough: COPYRIGHT SHOULD NOT BE ASSIGNED UNLESS THERE IS NO OTHER OPTION.

Loss of Control
The point has already been made that the photographer will lose control of their work and the way in which it is circulated. This means that the photograph could be used in association with a product of which the photographer does not approve, or in association with a political party or regime with which the photographer has no wish to be associated; or, a concern particularly where models have been used, the whole or part of the photograph could be used out of its original agreed context.

Potential Value of Copyright
The fee for an assignment of copyright should be equal to a lifetime's use of the image in every context, but clients are rarely willing or able to pay the level of fee which an assignment is worth, and it is very difficult to work out a fee for something which includes all forms of use yet to be invented, appearing anywhere in hyperspace.

Example Take a commission for a photograph for a minor use, such as a one-off trade advertisement, for which the photographer will charge an appropriately small fee. The client order which accompanies the commission may demand an assignment of copyright. Clients should recognise that there is a great deal of difference between the use of a one-off trade advertisement and the potential opportunities for use represented in an assignment of copyright. The chances of a campaign becoming so successful that world wide, all media usage by the client becomes a reality, is something which is better tackled as and when the need arises. This is something which some clients find difficult to understand, and so rights granted should be clearly outlined and agreed before a job is confirmed.

Secondary Rights

It is increasingly important to hold on to copyright because of an area of rights known as 'Secondary Rights'. These are rights which are difficult or impossible for the creator to administer themselves on an individual basis. They are normally administered collectively through a collecting society, and the collecting society is responsible for distributing revenue to artists and photographers. The Design and Artists Copyright Society (DACS) is the copyright and collecting society for visual artists (including photographers) in the UK.

If the photographer assigns their copyright, then there will be no secondary rights for DACS to administer on their behalf and photographers, unlike all other types of creators, will receive nothing for these uses (u10:e3:p84).

The Main Terms of the Licence

The licence which the photographer, as the copyright owner, grants to their client, should reiterate the terms and conditions of business which were established in the estimate. Before moral rights were incorporated into UK copyright law, photographers used the terms of business established at the estimate stage and accepted by the client to ensure that clients gave credits where required and to ensure that works were not excessively cropped or manipulated. This is still a useful way of reinforcing the protection afforded by moral rights. Also covered in the licence are exclusivity and any confidentiality needs which the client may have. Apart from these, there are a number of basic points which must be covered by the licence, and the following should provide a useful check list, though it isn't an exhaustive one (see *ill 3:p109*)

Term of Licence	How long does the client wish to reproduce the photograph for? eg.1 year, 3 years, or more?
Media	Where can the client reproduce the photograph? eg. one insertion only, press campaign, posters, point of sale, showcard, advertising, editorial.
Territory	Where will the client have the right to reproduce the work? eg. UK only, Europe, Worldwide, English Language publications only?
Quantity	How many copies will be made? eg. 20,000 A2 posters, 50,000 CD-ROM, the normal circulation of 'X' magazine.
Edition	If the photograph is to appear in a book, will the licence apply for the first edition only or beyond?

Exclusive Licence

For photographers and their clients, an exclusive licence serves two purposes. It is a very practical contractual term which grants the client exclusivity, either for an agreed time period, for a particular use, or in association with a particular type of product. For example, the client may ask that a photograph they have commissioned for use in a shampoo advertisement is never resold by the photographer in association with any other product of that type.

Such forms of client exclusivity are very important for advertising photography where commercial considerations of this kind are an essential part of the arrangement.

Exclusive licences have a second, and perhaps more fundamental purpose, which carries legal weight and enables the exclusive licensee, ie. the client, to take legal proceedings should a third party infringe the copyright in the work. This is very useful for clients because the photographer, as copyright owner, may be unable or unwilling to pursue a breach of copyright on behalf of the client.

An exclusive licence must be in writing, signed by the copyright owner, to the exclusion of anyone else, including the copyright owner themselves. Exclusivity can be limited to specifics, eg. time period or type of use, or territory. The form of the exclusive licence is important and the copyright owner/photographer who wishes to use the work themselves during the period of exclusivity, for example by including it in their portfolio, should ensure that the client grants back to them a licence for this purpose.

Clients sometimes insist on an assignment of copyright because they wish to be in a position to take proceedings for infringements, for example if the photograph is used by a competitor. By granting the client an exclusive licence, the photographer avoids the need to assign copyright; the client can sue in their own right.

ELEMENT 5 : THE COMMISSIONED PHOTOGRAPHER AND COPYRIGHT

A commissioned photographer is normally a freelance photographer who is commissioned on a job-by-job basis to complete particular commissions on behalf of a number of different clients. This is the way in which most professional photographers work. They are the first owners of the copyright in their photographs, and the agreements which they conclude and the licences which they, or their agents, grant to the client, have a direct bearing on their ability to earn a living. Different types of photographers use their rights and earn their livings from them in different ways.

Advertising Photographers

A large percentage of the income of an advertising photographer comes from the first use of the photograph, for which they are paid a fee for their time and their creativity. In the UK this fee normally includes the first use of the work for which a licence is granted, and the photographer is also paid separately for the expenses of the job. If the first campaign is successful, the photographer may be asked to issue further licences for an extended time period or additional media, for which additional usage fees are paid by the client. When the licence period is complete and as long as the photographer respects fully both the client's rights and requirements (eg. agreeing never to sell a commissioned shot to a competitor of the client) and the rights of any third parties appearing in the photograph (eg. the model), then the photographer may be in a position to earn further income from the photograph by placing it with a photographic library.

Editorial Photographers

In the past, editorial clients commissioned photography on the basis of 'First British Use Only', that is, the photographer granted a licence to publish the photograph for the first time, and once only, in the UK. Now that the UK is part of the European Union, this is changing, but the principle remains the same. The majority of publishers run in-house syndication agencies and, as part of the agreement with the publisher, the photographer may permit their photographs to be syndicated and share fees from syndication with the publisher client. Sometimes photographs will sell better if they are syndicated along with the article, and so the photographer will earn more this way. However, many in-house syndication agencies are not active in promoting the photographer's work and prefer to wait for business to come to them. Photographers may feel it is better to syndicate their work themselves, or through a picture library or agency which will be active in promoting their work to potential clients.

Taking the Long Term View

Whether advertising or editorial, photography can be a lonely profession, and photographers are vulnerable to pressure from clients who, are increasingly coming to recognise the value of copyright without being prepared to pay for it. Like other creators, photographers are in most instances going to be the weaker party in any negotiation because they are dependent on their clients for work and for payment. In addition, individual freelancers don't have the legal and business back-up which publishers and advertising agencies have.

Young photographers should be aware that some clients will, amongst other things, press for an assignment of copyright, and while looking for short term opportunities to enter the industry, photographers should be aware that, in the long term, holding on to their rights and learning the business skills associated with photography is the only way to survive in the industry.

Photographers should join those trade associations and trade unions which have been set up for them. The social contact gained from such organisations removes the feeling of isolation, and provides the kind of back-up to the photographer which publishers and other clients treat as a matter of course.

ELEMENT 6 : THE NON-COMMISSIONED/LIBRARY PHOTOGRAPHER

There are some, though not many, photographers who are able to make a living solely from their stock material, gallery sales or self-published books. They still have to protect their rights and the best way to do so is to ensure their paperwork is watertight and to have a good grasp of copyright and licensing. For such photographers to survive, they have to be good salespeople, good negotiators and good business men or women. Working through a library or agency can help, particularly where the agency acts as a co-operative, with photographers providing each other with mutual support and encouragement. Many of the most successful of these photographers are those who have gained experience, established a reputation, acquired a regular clientele and built up a library of photographs by working first on commission. It is only when they have done this that they are free to choose their own way of working.

For more information on photographers and their relationship with agencies, agents and stock libraries see u4:e9:p46. The professional organisation representing libraries and agencies is the British Association of Picture Libraries and Agencies (BAPLA).

ELEMENT 7 : COPYRIGHT AND THE STUDENT

When students are accepted on a course, they are normally required to sign an agreement with the college. As with any other agreement the student should read this document carefully, as it may contain an assignment of copyright covering every work which the student produces whilst at the college - even non course work! The practice of insisting on an assignment from creators at this early stage in their career, in exchange for education, is unfair and unreasonable. It is also a matter of concern that students are being taught poor business practice by those responsible for training in what is largely a vocational field.

It is understood that colleges need to be able to use student work in exhibitions and promotions of the college, and in some instances work may be included in brochures or leaflets. Instead of an assignment, the student should be asked to provide a licence for the very specific types of use which the college needs. The Association of Photographers is actively encouraging colleges to change the practice of demanding copyright assignments from students.

Students in college do need to work with, and learn from, the copyright works of other artists. This has been part of teaching practice for hundreds of years. However, with developments in technology and modern art practice, it has become increasingly easy and tempting to reproduce the works of other artists. The original artist or photographer may be prepared to accept use of their work within a college as part of the learning process. They will be less happy to see its continued presence in a portfolio once a student has left college. It is more professional and much less likely to cause difficulty later, if the student obtains permission before reproducing the copyright works of others.

Most creators are sympathetic and would wish to encourage students to analyse and discuss their work. What they don't want to see is a work which includes a reproduction of something they created being exhibited for sale in a gallery, perhaps in a mutilated or adapted form and carrying someone else's name. As educational users and as creators, students should be aware of the problems from both sides and should be encouraged to discuss the need to protect and respect creative works whilst exploring and analysing it for themselves.

ELEMENT 8 : FAIR DEALING AND OTHER PERMITTED ACTS

Under the 1988 Act, there are a number of ways in which copyright protected material may be used, without obtaining the consent of the copyright owner and without payment, although in some cases the copyright owner must be credited. Some of these involve a concept known as 'fair dealing'. 'Fair dealing' is a difficult term to explain as there is no satisfactory definition of the term and what is considered 'fair' depends on a number of factors.

The way in which the fair dealing sections of the 1988 Act affect the photographer depends on whether it is their own work which is being 'dealt' with or whether they are incorporating someone else's work into their own. The main categories of 'fair dealing' are listed below along with an explanation. In addition to these there are a number of 'permitted acts' which are not directly covered by the term 'fair dealing', but are things which can be done to a copyright work without infringing copyright.

News Reporting and Current Events

Although other artistic works may be 'dealt' with for the purposes of news reporting and current events, photographs may not be. To report current events, such as the theft of a famous painting, it may be desirable to show a picture of that painting, so fair dealing is acceptable in these circumstances. However, to permit the free use of photographs of a sports event or a news scoop, would mean that sports and news photographers would rarely be paid for their work and could not preserve 'exclusive' agreements with their publisher clients. Other newspapers would, in practice, be free to lift the images.

Criticism and Review

A photograph may be used for the purpose of criticism or review of the photograph or of another copyright work, provided the photographer is credited. Criticism and review do not apply in the context of photographic works being used in college for educational purposes.

Research and Private Study

Fair dealing with a work for the purpose of research and private study can apply for educational uses, but only if the student or the tutor make a single copy, and this may only be made during the course of study to which the copy of the photograph relates. In addition, such a copy may not be made by a reprographic process (eg. photocopying, slide or other photographic process). Therefore, in most instances, copies of photographs and other artistic works may not be made legally without the permission of the photographer or other creator.

Educational Use

Again, copies made by a reprographic process are not covered under this heading, unless they are made for the purposes of exams. It should be noted that copies made for examinations, which are subsequently dealt with in any other way, are immediately treated as infringing copies.

Libraries and Archives

These provisions are very specialised and relate to copies which the librarian makes on behalf of a tutor or student. On the whole, they do not apply to artistic works and photographs.

Librarians are strictly bound by these rules, which is why they may on occasion refuse to make copies requested by students and tutors. For more information on these speak to the college librarian.

Off-Air Recording of Television Programmes

The 1988 Act permits home copying of television programmes for the purpose of time shifting, but this does not cover the recording of such programmes for educational use.

However, provision for educational recording has been made through a licensing scheme run by the Educational Recording Agency (ERA) acting on behalf of broadcasters and other rights holders, including DACS for visual artists and photographers. More information on ERA is given on page 148 under the heading Useful Addresses.

Reprographic Copying - Photocopying and Slide Collections

Many educational establishments make photocopies of text from books and periodicals under a licensing scheme operated by the Copyright Licensing Agency (CLA). This scheme does not cover artistic or photographic works and photocopies of these works may not be made unless they fall under fair dealing provisions (eg. for the purpose of examination) or unless the permission of the photographer or artist has been obtained first.

DACS operates a licensing scheme for slide collections in educational establishments, which permits establishments to make slides from artistic works and photographs for educational use only. More information on DACS is available on page 85.

Incidental Inclusion

If a photograph has been used in a work produced by someone else, the photographer must decide whether that use is incidental. To make that decision, a number of points must be considered:

- is the whole or part of the photograph used?
- is it a significant part or a minor part of the photograph (eg. a key element)?
- does the use of the photograph enhance the work in which it appears?
- does the use of the photograph endorse a product?
- is the photograph there purely by chance?

It is perhaps easier to look at incidental inclusion from the point of view of the photographer incorporating someone else's work into their own and by taking some specific examples.

Example A If a portrait photographer is working in someone's home and in the background a portion of a painting can be seen. It is likely that this would be treated as incidental use. However, if the photographer has deliberately positioned the subject in front of the painting to make the photograph more attractive, then it is unlikely to be treated as incidental.

Example B A stylist working for a room-set photographer selects a painting and then dresses a set around that painting. Clearly the painting is a major decorative feature of the room and the photograph has been built around it. This is not incidental use and, for any such use, permission should be obtained and payment made first.

Example C A client from a furniture company wants his product associated with quality and the photographer is asked to photograph a chair by Le Corbusier next to a sofa made by the client. The copyline reads 'Quality speaks for itself'. The Le Corbusier chair has been used to endorse the client's product and to associate the qualities of the one with the other. This is not incidental use, and permission should be obtained and payment made first.

Permission may sometimes be necessary when incorporating trade marks and logos into photographs, particularly advertising photographs (u4:e3:p43).

Advertising the Sale of a Photographic Work

This section of the 1988 Act permits a gallery or saleroom to include a photograph in a catalogue or sale book, but only if the photograph is for sale. If, after the sale, the gallery continues to sell the catalogue to the public, this is not for the purpose of advertising the work for sale, and is not permitted.

ELEMENT 9 : RIGHTS IN UNDERLYING WORKS

Collage

Incorporating another photographer or artist's work in a collage or montage is not a breach of copyright if the material is clipped from newspapers or other publications. However, if the material is photocopied and then clipped, it is a breach of copyright because a reproduction has been made. The problem is more likely to arise if the collage itself is reproduced, for example in a photograph taken for publicity purposes. The original works will also be reproduced, so copyright will be breached.

For any artists working with collages, a knowledge of copyright in existing photographs will be useful and may help identify which photographs or other images are out of copyright and whether permission is needed for the remainder.

Some believe that the inclusion of parts of copyright works in a collage may be an infringement of the original artist's or photographer's moral rights.

Copyright in Photographs of Other Protected Works

When a photographer takes a photograph of a work which is protected by copyright, permission should first be sought for that photograph to be taken. It is a reproduction of the original work. Misunderstanding often arises with photographs of other artistic works, eg. photographs of three dimensional objects such as works of sculpture. The resulting photographic work probably carries copyright protection as an original work itself, but this does not negate the copyright in the underlying artistic work included in that photograph. Whilst the photographer may have been given permission to take the photograph, this does not mean they can permit others to make copies from it, and the photographer should always make this clear when loaning transparencies for publication purposes.

Example: A photographer with a picture library is asked by a well known ceramicist to take photographs of his latest collection of pots (works of artistic craftsmanship). Their agreement is that the ceramicist may use the photographs in his exhibition catalogue. The photographer is paid film, processing, print and travel costs. In exchange for her time and expertise, the photographer may include the photographs in her portfolio.

If the ceramicist is subsequently approached by a consumer magazine which wants to use the photographs in a feature, then permission is needed from the photographer first. Alternatively, if the photographer puts the photographs in her library, then all potential customers should be made aware that the permission of the ceramicist is needed before any reproduction of the photographs containing the pots can be made.

Certain Artistic Works on Public Display

There is a section in the 1988 Act which permits photographs to be taken of the following artistic works:

- a building;
- sculptures, models for buildings and works of artistic craftsmanship permanently situated in a public place or in premises open to the public.

A building which is a work of architecture may be freely photographed and that photograph reproduced; however the model for that work of architecture can only be photographed if it is permanently situated in a public place or in premises open to the public. The architect's drawings for the same building may not be photographed without the permission of the architect.

Perhaps the most important part of this section is that relating to works of sculpture. This section does not apply to works included in a temporary or travelling exhibition or where the sculpture is situated in a private garden or house.

The Publisher's Right

There are a number of misunderstandings about what rights a publisher owns in a published photograph or artistic work. The 'publisher's right', as it is known, relates to the right which exists in the typographic arrangement of the work, that is in the printed text of the book. There is no typographical arrangement of a photograph or illustration and thus there is no automatic 'publisher's right' in a photograph as there would be in a published edition of an author's work.

Publishers can and do acquire rights from photographers. Photographers should licence their works to publishers and not assign them.

ELEMENT 10 : INFRINGEMENT OF COPYRIGHT AND REMEDIES

Many of the problems which photographers have are not straightforward infringements of copyright. It is more likely that the photographer has completed a commission but has not been paid, even though the work has been used. The difficulties faced in pursuing a legal case against the commissioner or user are more likely to be of a contractual nature, but nevertheless, the implications of a case being brought against them for infringement of copyright are normally sufficient to persuade the client that the photographer should be paid.

On the other hand, it can be very expensive for the photographer to obtain specialist legal advice, to get letters written and to issue writs. Once again, watertight contractual conditions and approval from the client at every stage of the work, make it easier and cheaper for the photographer should non-payment occur and arguments arise (u3:e9:p36).

Where there is a straight forward infringement by a publisher, advertising agency or direct client, through inefficiency or ignorance, then the photographer may be willing to licence retrospectively, at a fee similar to that which they would have charged if permission had been sought before the reproduction was made.

Very few cases for infringement of a photographer's copyright actually get to court; most are settled out of court once the infringing user becomes aware of the full costs they will incur in defending the case. Also, when there is only a small amount of money involved, the photographer may feel that, in legal terms, it is not worth pursuing via a solicitor and may let the case drop.

It is possible for the photographer to pursue minor claims for copyright infringement through the small claims courts, the County Courts that is. However, as many county court judges are unused to dealing with such issues in these courts, the case needs to be straight forward and the photographer should have every piece of paperwork in order first and be prepared to make a clear and concise case.

Cases for infringement of copyright can be pursued through Civil or, in some cases, Criminal Law. A case may be brought by the copyright owner (the photographer), their heirs, or an exclusive licensee (u1:e4d:p18). The 'remedies' which the photographer can expect to receive from both the High and County Court are:

- Injunction - this will prevent the copying from taking place or from continuing;
- Account of Profits - the infringing user will have to provide details of the profits they have made from the illegal copies;
- Delivery Up - the infringing copies will be destroyed or handed over to the copyright owner;
- Damages;
- Additional Damages - which can be given for flagrant infringements.

The copyright owner does not have to prove the infringer knew the work was protected; the act of infringement is enough.

The alternative to Civil Proceedings is to take the case to the Criminal Courts. The photographer would need to retain a solicitor, but such cases are generally dealt with more quickly than civil proceedings. Use of the Criminal Courts is increasing, but can be difficult because courts are not yet used to dealing with Copyright. No damages are awarded under a criminal prosecution, only fines, and in certain cases compensation. The level of proof demanded in the Criminal Courts will be higher than that required by the Civil Courts.

A case may be brought against anyone with sufficient knowledge of an infringing act of a criminal nature which they know or have reason to believe has taken place. The criminal acts are phrased differently to the civil ones, but in general it is obvious that they are infringements eg. making copies for sale or hire; selling or letting for hire commercially;

offering or exhibiting for hire commercially; possessing for commercial purposes; importing into the UK for commercial purposes; distributing non-commercially so as to cause economic damage to the copyright owner.

Photographers should, wherever possible, ensure their name appears on originals and on licensed copies of their work, as this can be important if it becomes necessary to prove authorship of photographs when pursuing a case for infringement of copyright.

SUMMARY

Copyright law in the UK has been around since the 18th Century and photography for over 150 years. Yet, prior to the 1988 Copyright, Design & Patents Act coming into force, photographers did not have control over where or how their commissioned work was used. They received no further income from it, and could not bequeath it to their heirs. Now it is yours to control, and it will continue for seventy years after your death. It was a long time coming and should be understood and respected as your right by law.

Unit 2 : Moral Rights

INTRODUCTION

Moral rights are an intrinsic part of copyright, but they are different from other aspects of copyright law because they are not 'economic rights', that is they have no direct financial value. However, they acquire economic value because they are included in the negotiating process and because failure to respect moral rights can result in financial penalties.

More important to many photographers is the fact that moral rights give them the same right to respect for their work that other creators have, and therefore acknowledges the photographer's right to be treated as any other creator.

Unit 2 provides information on the different moral rights and how these are applied in professional practice. Photographers are encouraged to use their moral rights and to respect the moral rights of other creators, and also to understand the importance and relevance of these rights to their creativity and to the integrity of their work.

ELEMENT 1 : WHAT ARE MORAL RIGHTS?

As already mentioned in the Unit on Copyright, moral rights are part of the Universal Declaration of Human Rights.

As well as protecting the creator's economic rights (ie. copyright), creative works such as photographs, paintings, writing and music, reflect their creator's personality and so they must be more highly valued and respected than other forms of physical property. These rights are the 'moral rights', a term which emphasises the importance of maintaining the integrity and inviolability of the work, rather than its economic value. Like copyright, moral rights can be legally enforced (where the right is upheld the author is entitled to remedy, which may be financial), and therefore they do have economic value in negotiations.

Moral rights should not be confused with moral and ethical issues, which in this publication are covered under Unit 4 - Ethics (Principles of Best Practice).

In the UK as elsewhere in Europe, moral rights are an integral part of copyright law, but in the UK moral rights for authors were introduced into legislation for the first time in the 1988 Act. Moral rights are rights which are said to be 'personal' rights, that is they are granted to the photographer and cannot be transferred, unlike copyright which can be assigned. This means that the photographer can only exert or assert the moral rights or give them up (a waiver), no one else (other than the photographer's heirs) can benefit from the protection which these rights afford to the work of the photographer.

ELEMENT 2 : KEY POINTS

The four key moral rights are:

a) The right to be identified as the author or director, known as the 'Paternity Right'

This is the photographer's right to have their name appear alongside their photograph and to be associated with their photograph whenever it appears. In the photographic world the term normally used is 'by-line' or 'credit'. The right applies in the following circumstances: when a photograph is published; when it is exhibited in public; when it is broadcast; or when it appears in a film. The identification should be clear and reasonably prominent. Unfortunately, there is a long list of exceptions to which the right does not apply and the three most important of these for photographers are:

i) for the purpose of reporting current events;
ii) for publication in newspaper, magazine or similar periodical, or a 'collective work of reference' (this means publications such as encyclopedias or dictionaries).
iii) to employees for works made during the course of their employment.

Before the introduction of the 1988 Act, established trade practice meant that photographers were credited for work which appeared in an editorial context but not for work used for advertising or promotional purposes. Trade practice has now been turned on its head and a photographer is theoretically entitled to a credit on an advertisement hoarding but not on a portrait in a newspaper.

The right to be identified as the author only applies if it is asserted 'by an instrument in writing'. This means that a statement to the effect that the right has been asserted should be written and signed by the photographer. The current practice of putting the international copyright symbol, the photographer's name and the year of creation on a print is not sufficient for an assertion; it should also include a statement that the right has been asserted, and the signature of the photographer. Photographers, like writers, should ensure that an assertion of this right appears in the front of any published edition in which their work appears (u1:e3:p16).

Where an assignment of copyright is made, the photographer should ensure that an assertion of the right to be identified is included in the assignment. Similarly, the assertion should be written into the terms and conditions of any licence, both as a moral right and, where the right does not exist (where there is an exclusion), the contractual term will enforce the photographer's right to a credit and their right to protect the integrity of their work, and certainly, in the case of a right to a credit, it supports existing trade practice in many areas.

Asserting the right to be identified in relation to the public exhibition of a photograph, means ensuring that the photographer is identified on the original or copy, or on the mount. This will bind anyone who comes into contact with that original or copy, irrespective of whether the assertion is visible or still present. There are no specific requirements as to how this type of assertion should be made. It is also possible to assert this right through the licence or agreement which permits the making of limited editions of prints and, again, it is probably a good idea to make the moral right or credit part of the contractual arrangement with any gallery exhibiting a photographer's work. Not only does this mean that the photographer's name appears on the wall of the gallery next to their photographs, but it will also ensure that they have a credit should the photograph be used on any publicity associated with the exhibition.

b) The right to object to derogatory treatment of a work - known as the 'Integrity Right'

'Derogatory treatment' includes any addition to, deletion from, alteration to, or adaptation of the photograph, which is also derogatory. In the words of the 1988 Act, 'derogatory' means a distortion or mutilation of the photograph, or some other treatment prejudicial to the honour or reputation of the photographer. Most of these descriptions are emotive and depend very much on the interpretation afforded to them.

For example, in a cigarette advertisement with the Pyramids as a background, it may be perfectly acceptable to the photographer that the Pyramids are manipulated together to provide an image which fits the shape of the final advertisement (although some photographers may prefer to supervise or carry out the manipulation of their work themselves). However, if the image is to be used in an editorial context, the photographer may feel that tampering with a similar shot of the Pyramids, for the sake of composition on the printed page, damages the integrity of their shot and thus their reputation.

This right is an automatic right and does not need to be asserted.

The Integrity Right applies in the same circumstances as those in which the paternity right applies. There is also a similar set of exceptions to those which apply to the Paternity Right. Again, it is for the photographer to ensure, through the use of contractual clauses, that their work gets the respect it deserves in these situations.

c) The right not to have a work falsely attributed to a person as its author or director - known as the 'False Attribution Right'

The false attribution right existed under the 1956 Act, and is a right which belongs not to the author, but to anyone who wrongly has a work attributed to them. However, for the photographer it most often arises when their name is put onto someone else's work.

This may seem obscure and unlikely, but it does happen, for example where a promotional publication has prepared artwork for the advertisements of two photographers and the names have been transposed under the artworks. Or, it could happen deliberately, where an advertiser wishes to use a photographer's name for endorsement value but cannot afford the photographer's fees.

The right is automatic and does not need to be asserted. It applies in similar circumstances to those outlined for other moral rights. There are no exceptions to this right.

d) The right to privacy in respect of certain photographs and films - known as the 'Privacy Right'

There is no general law of privacy in the UK (u4:e1:p41). The section of the 1956 Act which granted copyright to the commissioner of a photograph or of a painted portrait was, in some ways, an early and largely ineffectual attempt to combine copyright with privacy. It failed because, increasingly, those who controlled copyright and commissioned photographs were the media (normally the exploiters of photographs). Under the 1988 Act, the first owner of copyright is the photographer, so legislators felt that there should be some way of controlling the dissemination and publication of private photographs, and indeed films, by unscrupulous photographers or media.

The important point to note about the wording of this moral right, is that it applies only to commissions for 'private and domestic purposes', for example, wedding photographs and family portraits - social photography in fact. It is not intended to cover photographs taken in the home of an actor or actress who has commissioned the portrait for their portfolio, or those commissioned by a Sunday supplement, such as 'A Room of My Own'; these are 'for use in the course of business' and are not protected by the Privacy Right.

The photographer is normally the copyright owner of photographs commissioned for private and domestic purposes, but the commissioner has the right to prevent copies of the photograph from being issued to the public, or broadcast, or exhibited or shown in public - and that includes the high street shop window of the social photographer (although most people, if asked, are delighted to see their image reproduced and displayed in this way).

ELEMENT 3 : DURATION OF MORAL RIGHTS

Moral rights apply to the work of any photographer who was alive on or after the 1st August 1989; whether the work was created before that date or after is irrelevant.

Moral rights last for the same length of time as copyright, that is life of the photographer plus 70 years, apart from the False Attribution Right which lasts for life plus twenty years.

Again the new regulations create additional complications for photographers. As moral rights did not exist in the UK before August 1st 1989, they would not apply to most revived copyright works, the possible exception being photographs. Some photographs taken before 1945 (see u1:e2g:p15) were taken by photographers who were still alive in 1989, or indeed are still alive now (assuming that for the purposes of the duration of copyright, protection will be determined in accordance with the 1988 Act). They may therefore be entitled to moral rights in at least some of their works.

ELEMENT 4 : CONSENT AND WAIVER OF MORAL RIGHTS

Moral rights may not be assigned to another person or company; they apply only to the creator or their heirs. However, it is not illegal for someone to do something to a photographer's work if they have the photographer's consent. That consent should normally be given in writing, but the consent can be spoken or by implication, that is if the photographer has given consent for a previous commission and has not amended their terms for the new commission. Obviously, written consent is much more satisfactory for those to whom the consent is granted.

Moral rights may also be waived. A waiver is normally made in writing by the photographer, but again it could be done orally, and is most often part of the contract into which the photographer enters with their client. A photographer should not waive their moral rights. Is it right that a client should expect a photographer to give up the right to be associated with their work or to prevent themselves from being falsely associated with someone else's work? Why would a photographer permit the mutilation of their work to the extent that it is damaging to their honour or reputation? Any photographer agreeing to a waiver should be very careful about its wording, in particular to the extent of the waiver, which should be very clear and precise to prevent it applying to all their works generally, or to a type of work, or to all existing or future works.

Where a waiver is required for the Paternity Right, it may be easier for the photographer to agree not to assert the right in that particular case. This is fairly common in the film industry, for example.

To prevent the photographer from being presented by their client with an unfavourable contract requiring a waiver, it is better to discuss the client's requirements beforehand and for the photographer to include the agreed terms in their contract. For example, where an advertising client wishes to manipulate an image for a particular effect.

Of course, enforcing moral rights through the courts is costly and difficult, but it is important that photographers do not waive these fundamental rights. The Writers Guild, Society of Authors and other groups, fought hard to see these rights established in British law and continue to fight against waivers. It would be a great pity if photographers did not equally value such hard fought for rights.

ELEMENT 5 : MORAL RIGHTS IN PRACTICE

Most of the relevant points of the practical application of moral rights have already been covered, but the following are the key points to remember:

- Moral rights should, wherever possible, be covered in the photographer's terms of business. In that way, moral rights are reinforced contractually and where they don't apply, the photographer introduces them as a purely contractual term which strengthens good trade practice (*ill 1:p106*).
- The Paternity Right does not apply unless it has been asserted by the photographer, normally in writing.
- Wherever possible, moral rights should not be waived. It is better for the photographer to identify their client's needs and consent to these in advance as part of the contract.
- Rather than waive rights, the photographer should agree not to assert the Paternity Right.
- If a waiver is unavoidable, then the photographer should ensure it is specific to the named photograph and in relation to the required use only. The photographer should put the waiver in writing and keep a copy of it on file.
- Photographers should encourage clients to agree to a revokable waiver, as this can be of benefit to the client as well as the photographer.

ELEMENT 6 : BREACH OF MORAL RIGHTS

Moral rights are not property rights, and so breaches of these rights are not treated in the same way as for infringement of copyright.

Cases for breach of moral rights may only be brought by the photographer, or his/her heirs, and these are acted on in the Civil Courts only. So far, in photography, the majority of cases have been settled out of court. Not surprisingly, photographers and their advisers have been unwilling to bring costly cases to court where the outcome is dependent on the court's interpretation of terms such as 'damage to honour or reputation' and 'derogatory treatment', and where the levels of damages are assessed on that interpretation. It is possible to pursue a breach of moral rights through the courts, and this will probably be done more frequently with the expansion in digital use and dissemination of works, with the increased likelihood of unauthorised manipulations of works circulating widely. It is increasingly important that photographers should know how to use and protect their moral rights.

Injunctions can be obtained against both anticipated and actual breaches of moral rights, preventing the reproduction of works or ensuring that breaches are corrected before the reproduction is distributed. With the Integrity Right it is possible to prohibit reproduction or agree to the inclusion of a disclaimer in the publication which disassociates the photographer from the treatment of the work. The photographer may also be compensated for damages, including irritation, loss of reputation and other non-monetary losses, but these can be very difficult to quantify unless the photographer can demonstrate damage to their career. If the photographer wins their case, then they may be in a position to recoup most of their legal costs from the infringer.

ELEMENT 7 : PHILOSOPHY OF MORAL RIGHTS

Moral Rights are a fundamental human right and represent the creator's contribution to the cultural and intellectual heritage of humanity.

UK Law (u1:e1:p11) is such that the worth of copyright works is seen to lie only in its exploitation, in its value as a commodity in the marketplace. This is the case whether it is young performers and musicians who are tied into onerous contracts before they've even begun to create, or artists whose works are resold for thousands on the fine art market, whilst the artists are unable to make more than a few pounds out of the first sale to a gallery.

Of course, these are extreme examples, but a world which values creations whilst forgetting the creator is not one in which a photographer can easily make a living. The European rule of Droit d'Auteur may not be perfect, but it goes some way towards redressing the balance, and other European photographers are much more aware of their rights and are willing to discuss them as issues which have a direct bearing on their creativity. It is this direct involvement and understanding of copyright and moral rights which needs to be fostered by students of photography, their tutors and working photographers alike.

Issues around the Integrity Right, such as appropriation, digital manipulation and modern art practice, need to be discussed and debated. Should moral rights be extended and strengthened, for example to prevent destruction of works, or just to ensure they are unwaivable? Can moral rights take on a new role in the digital environment or should they be abandoned?

These questions need to be discussed where it matters most, that is amongst the practitioners themselves, not just by professional bodies and legal advisers. Students in particular should be encouraged to discuss these issues now and to help form the type of legislation needed for the future.

SUMMARY

Moral rights are relatively new in the UK but they are of increasing importance to photographers. These rights are an integral part of the creative process of photography. An awareness of the application of moral rights and of the principles which underlie these rights will strengthen the position of the professional photographer for the future.

Unit 3 : Standards & Codes of Practice

INTRODUCTION

Sustaining a living as a photographer requires an applied knowledge of general business practice and also an understanding of standards specific to the photographic industry.

Standards and codes of practice are necessary in an industry where a small business deals with large corporations. Establishing good business ethics from the first commission gives a photographer the same standing and respect extended to large companies. To have everyone working to the same standards gives photography a strong voice and the respect it deserves. The following may appear to emphasise the business of an advertising photographer, but the basic principles apply to all areas of photography.

This Unit will encourage photographers to understand that accepted standards and codes of practice are intrinsic to making a business out of photography, and equip them with the necessary information to do so.

ELEMENT 1 : PORTFOLIO PRESENTATION

i) Portfolio cases should be distinctive, workable and well marked. Bigger is not better - a large heavy portfolio can be unmanageable and is less likely to be hauled up the stairs. Delivery should be accompanied by a standard Delivery Note (*ill 5:p113*) stating name, address, contents and purpose for presentation. Contents should not include original work - unless requested by the client.

ii) Responsibility for the folio and its contents rests with the agency/client from the time of delivery until its return to the photographer/agent. This is covered by the agency's or client's 'goods in trust' insurance (u9:e1j:p78), and a claim can be made should work be lost or damaged. However, a photographer should also have their own portfolio insurance (u9:e1i:p77).

iii) The portfolio should not be used by an agency in a 'pitch' unless representing the photographer. A pitch is when the agency is attempting to win a client's business for a specific product and presents a possible campaign using visuals. Permission must be given by the photographer before work is used for pitching and a fee may be charged for this.

ELEMENT 2 : FEES

There are no standard fees in photography and it is recommended that the client's budget is established before pricing of the job begins. Photographers' fees, or day rates, need to encompass not only their creativity, experience, specialisation and uniqueness, but also the tools of their trade. These include the cost of running a studio (heat, light, phones, full-time assistants, insurances, etc.), equipment purchases and maintenance. Location photographers will still need to maintain a base/office and this should be included. Work out all these amounts over a year and divide the total by the number of anticipated working days; this figure will represent the minimum fee required before charging for personal expertise. Editorial fees are generally set by the commissioning magazine (u5:e8b:p53).

ELEMENT 3 : PRE-PRODUCTION/EXPERIMENTAL & SPECULATIVE PHOTOGRAPHY

Some shoots may require extensive planning, location finding, model casting, pre-production meetings or consultations, and detailed quotes. Fees may be charged for these pre-production costs and should be agreed with the client in advance.

When the client does not know what use the finished work will be put to, they may commission on an experimental basis. Recommended trade practice is to charge a fee of 50% of the normal day rate plus expenses. The work should not be used by the photographer, client or models unless all parties agree. Any use by the client must then produce the other 50% of the fee. Agreements must be reached with any third parties involved in the shoot (eg. set builders, models, and stylists) with regard to payment, and re-negotiations may be necessary, particularly with models, if the work is subsequently used by the client.

Any work done on this basis for less than 50% of the fee is called speculative photography and is unethical, but a minimum payment of expenses should be claimed by a photographer who chooses to work on this basis. If the work runs, a full fee plus expenses should be paid.

ELEMENT 4 : BOOKINGS/ART ORDERS (See also u5:e1:p49 and u5:e3:p49)

Bookings can be oral or written, provisional or confirmed. If a photographer already has a provisional booking by another client, the first client should be given the opportunity to confirm and that booking should be honoured. Oral bookings should be followed up by an official art order from the agency/client, before the shoot begins, stating the following:

i) Client, product and agency
ii) Photographer, Art Order No., and date
iii) Format
iv) Agreed fee, Base Usage Rate (u5:e8a:p52, *ill 7:p117*), pre/post production fees
v) Media, territory, exclusivity & time period
vi) Expenses

Editorial commissions are generally made at short notice, but where possible the photographer should fax to the magazine a confirmation of their conversation, as orders will not normally arrive before the shoot starts. Where possible, request an art order to be faxed before the job commences. Proof of receipt, and sending, is recorded and printed out by the fax machine and should be kept with all other paperwork.

ELEMENT 5 : EXPENSES AND ADVANCES

Photographers are entitled to request up to 100% of reasonable estimated expenses in advance of large scale shoots, payable by the first day. On large scale overseas shoots commanding large up-front expenses, the photographer can expect to have the advance paid at least one month prior to commencement of the shoot.

Reasonable expenses should be agreed with the client, and are additional to the fee. They should not exceed the amount stated on the official art order. If, during the shoot, more expenses than agreed are required, the client contact (often an art director/art buyer) must be kept informed as they are incurred. Extra expenses are often at the request of the client, but approval should still be confirmed. Approval from the client should be sought at all times when purchasing props, etc. outright.

Model fees

Model fees include fitting, rates for additional usage and agency commission; model agencies charge 10 - 20% on top of the model's fee, so make sure this is in the budget. Child models require a casting fee. Where possible the client should pay the model agencies direct, but the booking of the models is generally done by the photographer on behalf of the client, although in some circumstances the agency/client will book the models direct and the photographer acts solely as a liaison for casting. Model fees are very specific to the usage, and care should be taken that this usage is the same as the photographer's (u3:e9d:p37).

Film and Processing charges

There are no standard rates for charging out film. Costs should not only be the basic film costs, but should include all film, including Polaroid, overtime, rush charges and professional laboratory rates. They should also reflect the costs of maintenance of the stock, storage, wastage, purchase and testing of batches of film to ensure continuity of emulsion. Many clients are requesting film and processing receipts, making it impossible for the costs to reflect these handling charges. Where possible film costs should not be shown as a specific item because this practice can lead to arguments as to who owns the actual negative or transparency. A charge for materials, which includes all these costs, could be shown on the final invoice. Arguments over the ownership of the film can make it difficult, at a later date, for the photographer to keep the originals in their possession. This in turn makes policing the use of the work almost impossible and could lead to copyright infringements (u1:e2e:p13).

Insurance (See Unit 9)
The cost of insurance policies including goods in trust, public and employer's liability, negative insurance, and loss/damage is normally reflected within the photographer's fee. Clients have the option of refusing to pay extra insurance premiums, eg. weather insurance. When a shoot is weather dependent, the client should be given the option of taking out weather insurance (u9:e1f:p76). This insurance is optional and can be costly, but its importance should be stressed.

Labour/Subcontractors
Fees for stylists, hairdressers, make-up artists, location finders, set builders and freelance assistants are all payable by the photographer and should be itemised fully and agreed with the client in advance.

Studio & equipment
Basic facilities are generally included in the photographer's fee, but, dependent on the type of photography, hire studios and special equipment may need to be itemised and charged for separately.

Props
The cost of hiring or purchasing props should be itemised, together with any insurance necessary for prop hire. If a stylist has been budgeted for, ensure that the stylist's time and any expenses incurred in securing props has been agreed with the client.

Transport and travel
Transport could include transportation of props and personnel, location vehicles, accommodation, subsistence (meals), and carnets. Carnets are necessary when equipment is being taken out of the country, and are basically a listing of the equipment being taken into other countries outside Europe. In countries outside the EU, that country's taxes will have to be paid on equipment where a carnet has not been completed. Carnets and advice are available from the London Chamber of Commerce (see Appendix). Mileage is generally charged at RAC or AA current rates, and figures are worked out on the cost of keeping a car on the road over a year. Both associations will supply these on request.

ELEMENT 6 : CANCELLATION AND POSTPONEMENT

Cancellation is when a shoot has been confirmed and is then abandoned and not re-booked. Cancellation fees are due only on confirmed bookings. The photographer will have booked time out to complete the work and may have turned down other work on the strength of it. Time will have been spent arranging assistants, models, film, equipment etc, so the photographer's time should be paid for. Ensure your terms and conditions state that you reserve the right to charge a cancellation fee - this can prevent argument later as it becomes a term of the contract, and not just industry practice. Any expenses already incurred should also be claimed.

General industry charges are as follows, but photographers may have different variations, (all days are working days):

Shoots of 2 days or less duration:

Within 2 days	100% fee + expenses
3 - 6 days	50% fee + expenses
7 days or over	25% fee + expenses

Shoots in excess of 2 days duration:

No. of shoot days or less	100% fee + expenses
Twice No. of shoot days	50% fee + expenses
Excess of twice shoot days	25% fee + expenses

Postponement is when a new date is given and confirmed, and fees may become payable to cover costs and inconvenience, but are at the photographer's discretion. However, expenses incurred which will have to be paid out again for the new shoot date should be paid in full.

Editorial work is more difficult for calculating cancellation fees, due to the short time span between commission and shoot. Very often the only payment will be actual expenses incurred, but some of the fee should also be claimed for.

Bookings which are dependant on weather conditions should be discussed with the client prior to the shoot, and weather insurance (u9:e1f:p76) can be taken out by the client and the premiums paid by them. Recommended trade practice is that 50% of the photographer's fee plus all expenses are payable on postponement due to bad weather.

ELEMENT 7 : REJECTION AND NON-USE OF WORK

Rejection

A representative of the client on the shoot, normally the Art Director, accepts or rejects the photography on behalf of the company. If they are present throughout, they will have seen the set, given and taken advice on the presentation of the subject matter and lighting, and been shown Polaroids indicating how the final shot will look. Contacts/film will have been looked at, discussed and the final images chosen. Acceptance by this representative is taken that the shoot has produced the agreed images and the photographer has kept their side of the bargain and completed their side of the contract. If no representative is present, then it is generally taken that the photographer's judgement is final.

Rejection after the shoot

If no representative of the client was present, and if a portfolio of the photographer's work was seen before the commission, then rejection of the work, on aesthetic grounds, is not acceptable. It could be presumed that no direction from, or on behalf of, the client gives the photographer the final say, and that the expertise of the photographer is sufficient. The photographer should be paid in full and should not be expected to subsidise any expenses of the shoot. Should a re-shoot be negotiated, new fees and expenses should also be negotiated.

Rejection of work on technical grounds

Work may be rejected for the following technical reasons:

i) Unacceptable quality of the transparency or print, eg. inappropriate or old film used.
ii) Technical failure by the photographer or any service for which it was agreed they were responsible.
iii) The photographer has not produced the details or effects as specified in the brief.

The photographer should be given the opportunity to re-shoot at their own expense. If a re-shoot is not offered or accepted, no fee is payable and any expenses paid in advance should be refunded.

Any rejection of work should be made within a maximum of 10 days from the date the film/contacts are delivered to the client.

Non usage of accepted work

Work that is accepted, then not used by the client, should be paid for in full.

ELEMENT 8 : LIABILITY OF WORK/MATERIALS

The photographer is responsible for the safety of the photographic materials until they are delivered to the client. Damage, prior to delivery to the client, would involve a re-shoot at the photographer's expense. Insurance can, and should, be taken out to cover the film through all its varying stages (u9:e1h:p77). Public and Employer's liability insurance should be held by every photographer (u9:e2:p79, u9:e3:p79).

ELEMENT 9 : PAPERWORK

Estimate *(ill 1:p105)*

Photographers do not normally "quote" for a job because it is impossible to give a firm figure and a quote is binding. Estimates are based on the information/brief originally supplied by the client and should include the following:

- Agency and Advertiser or Client
- Photographer
- Job description
- Media use/territory/time period
- Right to a credit
- Exclusivity
- Fees (to include the original use)
- Expenses
- Base Usage Rate (u5:e8a:p52, *ill 7:p117*)
- Contingency (10%)*
- Terms and Conditions printed on reverse.

*The contingency figure allows 10% to cover any unforeseen costings, enabling the client to allow for a possible extra charge over the estimated figure up to a maximum of 10%.

Invoice *(ill 2:p107)*

Invoices should follow the same format as the estimate, but without the contingency and less any advances paid. Terms and Conditions should always be printed on the reverse.

Correct and precise details with regard to the client, dates, and order numbers will help to ensure fast payment and are vital should the invoice not be paid and legal action for recovery is required. (Invoices for freelance assistants are covered in u3:e11:p39, *ill 4:p111*)

Licence *(ill 3:p109)*

The terms of the licence should have been negotiated at order and estimate stage and are what the fee has been based on. The layout of the licence is more specific than the estimate and invoice and should clearly show:

- Agency and advertiser or client
- Agency/client order No.
- Photographer job No.
- Date
- Photographer and agent
- Specific media (not just 'advertising'!)
- Particular country and language
- No. of years
- Exclusivity clause
- Description of the photograph
- Right to a credit

The licence period is deemed to start on the date of first insertion (when a campaign is first shown/magazine edition is first published) and the time period agreed will start from this date and not the date of the licence. The licence must be in writing and signed by the photographer. A copy should go to the agency on behalf of the photographer and an additional copy should accompany the invoice. Again, the terms and conditions should be printed on the reverse.

NB. The estimate, invoice and licence (above and illustrated) specify the words 'Agency and Advertiser'. Where the client is a Design Group, or there is no middle man, substitute the wording as appropriate. For specific information on editorial commissions see u5:e8b:p53.

Model Release Form *(ill 6:p115)*

It is important when using any models, whether professional or not, that the use the image is to be put to is understood by all concerned. Model Release Forms should be used and clearly define the fee, territory, time period and media. Copies should be given to both the client and the model. Large model agencies advise their models not to sign releases, and so in these cases ensure the booking/confirmation form, given by the model agency, states the correct use as agreed.

It is important that the agency/client knows how, where and when the model agency will allow the model's image to be used. Should the client use the work for a different purpose than originally agreed, the model agency will look to the photographer for extra payment. Where possible, further usage should be negotiated by the client directly with the model agency and it is strongly advised that photographers do not get involved. Usage fees for models are dependant on the amount of exposure the model's image is to receive. Extensive exposure of a model using a particular brand will narrow their market for further work with other brand products and re-usage negotiations may be based on this fact. The client is best placed to agree extended use.

Work placed with a stock library should normally have paperwork showing that the models, whether professional or the general public, have agreed to the image being used. Laws of Privacy exist in almost every other country, but not in the UK, so care should be taken when using members of the public in any image used for advertising purposes (u4:e1:p41). Stock libraries generally will not accept work that does not have clearance by the people within the image.

Delivery Note *(ill 5:p113)*

A delivery note should be used whenever work (transparencies, negs etc) is sent to another party. It is a list of the images and states the terms and conditions under which the work is being submitted. It is an important document in that, should any work be lost or damaged, it clearly states the receiver's liability. Amongst many other things, the form also states that the work cannot be used or stored electronically without the photographer's permission.

ELEMENT 10 : PAYMENT

Payment from the agency is expected within 30 days from the date of the invoice. Invoices should be submitted promptly and interest can be charged on overdue accounts (general trade practice charges at the rates used by the major credit cards or the country's rate of inflation). If an invoice is not queried within 10 days it can be deemed as accepted.

It should be noted that, at the time of writing, legislation concerning interest is still being investigated by the government, and discussed with small businesses. If adopted it will give a legal right for all businesses to have the option to recover interest on all unpaid debts after the payment terms have expired. It will make charging interest a more viable proposition for small businesses.

ELEMENT 11 : FREELANCE ASSISTANTS

Assisting Photographers

The Association of Photographers is actively championing a change in profile for 'freelance assistants', particularly those who have a wealth of experience and bring more to a shoot than just a helping hand. Most are already shooting for themselves, actively building up their portfolios and marketing themselves. It is much more a profession in its own right working 'with' the photographer, as oppose to 'for' them, using their expertise to work with only the direction required for the specifics of the shoot.

The first step was to change the name to 'Assisting Photographers' and freelancers are encouraged to print their business cards to reflect this change. To present a more professional look, The Association has produced invoice pads specifically designed to show all the necessary information, including the Schedule D No. required for the Inland Revenue (*ill 4:p111*). The bottom of the invoice refers to the following guidelines, which provide a code of practice between the photographer and the assisting photographer. These guidelines should be sent, before the shoot, to the photographer in order for them to become part of the contract between the two parties.

The following should be regarded as a guideline only, as photographers and assisting photographers (referred to here as 'assistants') may have their own terms of business. Any terms should be agreed between both parties before confirming bookings.

Bookings

Bookings are usually verbal and both photographer and assistant should understand if the work is provisional or confirmed. On confirmation the following should be agreed:

- Dates, start times, and daily hours
- Venue and travel arrangements
- Special requirements (clothing, equipment knowledge, etc.)
- Fee
- Expenses and overtime (where appropriate)
- Weather contingency for location work
- Possible overlaps with assistant's other confirmed jobs
- Invoicing details (invoice client or photographer?)
- Contact names and numbers

If an assistant has a provisional booking with another photographer, that photographer must be given the option to confirm before another booking is accepted.

Cancellation and Postponement

Cancellation by an assistant is not acceptable without unavoidable reason, eg. illness, and the substitution of another assistant must not be made without the photographer's prior knowledge and consent. The photographer has the right to approve any replacement before commencement of the shoot.

Where a booking is confirmed which may overlap a previously confirmed job, the photographer must be informed immediately and given the option to book another assistant.

Cancellation fees for freelance assistants are only payable for confirmed bookings, although once the booking is confirmed, an assistant should not be cancelled unless the job itself is cancelled. Freelance assistants should be regarded as chargeable items, and therefore covered by expenses when the photographer is charging the client a cancellation fee. In the case of a postponement, where a new date is given and confirmed, fees may become payable to cover costs and inconvenience, by mutual agreement between the photographer and assistant.

Fees and Payment

These are charged at a daily rate. A normal day is any 9 hour period worked between 7am and 9pm, and rates are dependant on knowledge, experience, and the type of work the photographer is doing, eg. advertising or editorial. Overtime may be charged for weekends, public holidays and in addition to the standard 9 hours, at a rate previously agreed with the photographer.

Payment should be made at the end of the shoot unless otherwise agreed at the time of booking. If immediate payment is not agreed, then credit terms of 30 days should be the maximum given. Assistants should give an invoice (*ill 4:p111*) clearly stating the following:

- Assistant's name, address, and Tax Schedule D Number
- Shoot/booking dates
- Assistant's invoice number
- Photographer's name and order number
- Client/Agency/Product
- Fee
- Expenses itemised
- Total owed
- Payment terms
- VAT number (if registered)

All expenses incurred on behalf of the photographer or client should be agreed in advance and are payable immediately the shoot is completed. Fees and mileage for the use of an assistant's car should be agreed at the time of confirmation.

Location Work

The photographer is responsible for the cost of accommodation and meals whilst on location, but personal expenses (eg. telephone calls) are the responsibility of the assistant. Medical and travel insurance should be discussed with the photographer before the shoot begins.

Weather-permitting bookings should be agreed with the assistant at the time of confirmation, but postponement due to bad weather will result in the assistant, as a photographer's expense, being paid 50% of the fee. The photographer or the client may have weather insurance to cover these events.

SUMMARY

The 1988 Copyright Act has given photography its true recognition as an art form. It is now up to photographers and their associations to standardise and maintain good business practice.

Unit 4 : Ethics (Principles of Best Practice)

INTRODUCTION

This unit covers the principles by which any professional photographer should operate. The majority of these principles are not governed directly by law but are based on common sense, goodwill and best practice.

This unit encourages photographers to adopt a personal ethical code based on good practice as recognised by the industry. An understanding of the types of ethical issues and decisions they may face will help young photographers to avoid some of the messy and unpleasant confrontations occasionally seen in the industry, and which tend to result from ignorance rather than ill will on the part of the photographer or client.

ELEMENT 1 : PRIVACY

Earlier units mention that certain aspects of copyright and moral rights have been used to replace the privacy legislation in the UK (u3:e9d:p38).

In the USA and other countries, laws relating to privacy and publicity are used mainly by celebrities to protect their personal image and to enable them to exploit it. The UK has no such protection although it is possible that if, for example, you use the image of James Dean or Marilyn Monroe, you may find yourself pursued by their Estates and sued under American law if your works appear in the USA, and a case can be brought under US legislation.

Use of People in Advertisements

Codes governing the use of people in advertisements are produced by The Committee of Advertising Practice, and the Advertising Standards Authority (ASA) are responsible for ensuring the system works in the public interest. The following is the code to be followed when using people in an advertising context:

a) Advertisers are urged to obtain written permission in advance if they portray or refer to individuals or their identifiable possessions in any advertisement. Exceptions include most crowd scenes, portraying anyone who is the subject of the book or film being advertised and depicting property in general outdoor locations.
b) Advertisers who have not obtained prior permission from entertainers, politicians, sportsmen and others whose work gives them a high public profile, should ensure that they are not portrayed in an offensive or adverse way. Advertisments should not claim or imply an endorsement where none exists.
c) Prior permission may not be needed when the advertisement contains nothing that is inconsistent with the position or views of the person featured. Advertisers should be aware that individuals who do not wish to be associated with the advertised product may have a legal claim.
d) References to anyone who is deceased should be handled with particular care to avoid causing offence or distress.
e) References to members of the Royal family and the use of the Royal Arms and Emblems are not normally permitted; advertisers should consult the Lord Chamberlain's office. References to Royal Warrants should be checked with the Royal Warrant Holders Association.

If complaints are received, and subsequently upheld, the ASA may ask for the offending advertisement to be withdrawn.

Example Objections were made to a National press advertisement for a private health scheme that featured a photograph of Virginia Bottomley, with the headline "Unlike NHS patients, ours never suffered from this terrible pain". The complainants believed the headline to be an offensive personal attack that lacked taste. Ms Bottomley's permission had not been given and the ASA concluded that the advertisement portrayed her in an adverse way, in contravention of the codes. The advertisers were asked not to repeat the advertisement.

Defamation

In the UK, images of British personalities are often used in an advertising or promotional context, often humorously, and such personalities are normally seen as fair game for this sort of treatment. However, such use must still be done with care and the image of a personality should not be used in a way which suggests they endorse the product. Every individual, and not just personalities, have the right to protect themselves against defamation.

Example: A photographer takes a photograph of a street scene and that photograph is subsequently sold for use in an advertisement. The advertisement implies that the individual in the photograph is a criminal or junkie. That individual may well bring a claim for defamation against the agency and client, or even the photographer.

Model Release Forms

Model release forms were originally devised as a means of establishing a basic contract between a photographer and a professional model (*ill 6:p115*). They were intended to permit only those forms of exploitation of the model's image which had been paid for by the photographer or their client. They are often mentioned in relation to privacy, and it is often suggested that members of the public who appear in a photograph should sign such a form.

However, this is not the main purpose of a model release form, and it is often impractical to get several members of the public to sign long and complicated forms allowing the use of their image. Under current UK law, there should be no problem with using a photograph which includes a member of the public, unless their image is used in a defamatory way or is in contravention of the ASA codes (as outlined above). Obviously photographers shooting for advertising purposes, or for library stock which may be used to endorse products, should take greater care.

Possible Privacy Legislation

For the present, the idea of introducing privacy legislation in the UK has been postponed indefinitely. However, it is a popular issue with parliamentarians and, when raised, photographers should follow debates and keep themselves informed of any proposals for legislation. Privacy legislation will have an impact on photography, and photographers should be prepared to work with their professional associations and advisers to influence the form which any legislation takes.

ELEMENT 2 : TRESPASS

For most photographers, only a small section of the law of trespass will ever be of interest. At present there is nothing in the law which prevents a photographer from taking photographs whilst on private property. However, the more important issue is whether the photographer has permission to be on that private property in the first place; if not they are trespassing.

Taking Photographs in a Public Place

Shooting in a public place, or shooting from a public place into a private place (for example standing in a public street and photographing a house and its garden), is not normally a problem and permission is not needed. However, if the photographer is causing a public nuisance by blocking the traffic in the public road whilst taking the photograph, then there may be problems. This is why, when organising a shoot in a public place, it is wise to notify the police first and to stick to any recommendations they may make.

Permits

Parks, and particularly royal parks, eg. Hyde Park and Windsor Park, are private parks and a permit must be obtained before any shoot can take place in them. Similarly, owners of public monuments and private landowners will normally permit photography if asked and if a payment is made. With the exception of major product advertising, the National Trust does not charge for permission to shoot on its landscape and coastline properties, although photographers are advised to contact the National Trust Photographic Library, should they wish to take pictures of SSSI land (Sight of Specific Scientific Interest) or listed species. See also Appendix, page 147.

ELEMENT 3: TRADE MARKS, STAMPS AND MONEY

The use of trade marks which are registered in the UK is governed by the Trade Marks Act 1994. The shooting of trade marks is not an infringement in itself, but the context of how it is used may be. Care should be taken when a trade mark is to appear in an image which may be used for advertising purposes, as this could be an infringement. Trade marks would have to be registered in the country in which the image was to be shown, or be registered internationally, for there to be an infringement; but it would not be so easy to police if the image was placed in a picture library.

Example The Hollywood sign was used in an image advertising audio visual equipment. The advertisment was shown in the UK. A letter was received, by the photographer, from the American company who licence the rights to use the sign, demanding money and the withdrawal of the ad. It was subsequently discovered that the Hollywood sign was not a registered trade mark in the UK and no rights had been infringed. If the ad had been shown in the US there would have been a claim.

NB. This case occurred 2 years before this edition was written; the Hollywood sign is probably now registered in all countries where registration is possible!

Strict rules govern the use of bank notes, coins and stamps in photography and illustration. The Bank of England have copyright in their notes, but reproduction is also covered by the Forgery and Counterfeiting Act 1981. There are particular procedures to be followed when seeking permission to reproduce notes, which can be time consuming and cannot be skirted around. The size of reproduction, context, positioning, and wording on the note are all taken into consideration when the Bank of England considers requests. HM Treasury's permission must be gained before reproducing coins which are governed by the same Act.

The Post Office owns the copyright in the design of British postage stamps. Applications for permission must be made in writing, and a fee may be charged for each application received. Again, there is a strict code of how stamps may be shown, including size of reproduction, detail (no alterations), context, positioning and colour.

ELEMENT 4 : CONFIDENTIALITY

Advertising Photography

Every photographer should recognise the importance of client confidentiality. Problems of confidentiality arise most often in connection with advertising photography, where the photographer is working with a client on an unlaunched product which must be kept secret from competitors until the advertising campaign is launched.

The rights which the advertising client agrees with the photographer (in the licence to use granted by the photographer) normally include the exclusive right to publish the photograph for the first time.

Unfortunately there have been occasions when photographers, carried away with enthusiasm for their photographs, have sent out promotional mailings for themselves before the client's campaign has been launched. This may be commercially disastrous for the client, and it certainly is for the photographer.

Photographers should also remember that even talking about their latest shoot with friends can be a breach of client confidentiality.

Editorial Photography

Confidentiality is an entirely different issue for the editorial photographer and is more a matter of trust between the photographer and the subject of their photographs.

Example Nude shots of a model are taken early in his/her career when the model was not aware of the need for a model release form. The model later becomes famous and the photographer is approached to sell the shots to a tabloid newspaper. Is it acceptable, or even ethical, for the photographer to do so?

Many magazines argue that copyright in 'celebrity' portraits should lie with them, to prevent unwanted exploitation of the photograph. But when a photographer takes a portrait, they enter into a position of trust with their sitter, and a relationship exists between the sitter and the photographer, not with the magazine. The photographer is often asked to ensure that the photograph appears only in 'X' magazine and to check with the celebrity first before any further use is made of it. If copyright is assigned to the magazine then the photographer is no longer in a position to control its use.

If photographers do not respect the subjects of their photographs, or treat them fairly, then it is only to be expected that clients will insist on acquiring copyright and owning control of the photographs themselves.

ELEMENT 5 : PASSING OFF

Passing off arises when a trader uses a misrepresentation to take advantage of the reputation and goodwill of another trader, and cashes in on that goodwill and reputation to the detriment of the first. Passing off can overlap with some areas of copyright law. A claim for passing off is normally brought in the civil courts.

Photography

In photography, deliberate passing off rarely happens; when it does, in such a visually aware industry, it is invariably found out. The photographer responsible is treated with contempt, not just by other photographers but also by clients who don't like to be made fools of.

Example A photographer puts tear sheets (images in the context of an advertisement) of another photographer's work into their own portfolio, and shows the portfolio to potential clients; or a photographer includes a brochure in his/her portfolio implying to the client that all the photographs in a brochure are theirs and not just the shot on page 10.

Photographic Assistants

Photographic assistants, particularly in the advertising industry, work closely with the photographer and are often given a great deal of responsibility. Their position is one of trust which can easily be abused, mainly because the assistant has not fully thought through the consequences of their actions.

Example A photographic assistant who has worked on a shoot as senior assistant and may even, technically, have 'pressed the button', feels that their contribution is great enough for them to claim the photograph as their own and put it in their portfolio. Of course, the client was not theirs and they were not ultimately responsible for the costs, the organisation or the creative influence. To claim such shots as their own is unacceptable practice; it may well be fraudulent too.

Occasionally an assistant will use a photograph taken 'off the back' of a shoot, in their portfolio.

Example A photographic assistant goes to an exotic location with a car photographer and has the opportunity to borrow the car to take some pictures independently. In this case, the assistant should seek permission from the photographer and possibly the client first, particularly where a product is involved. If permission is given they should also be prepared to mention both the original car photographer and the client if the shot is included in their portfolio.

Where an assistant takes photographs on someone else's shoot, they should consider their image carefully and decide whether it is sufficiently different in style and technique to warrant its inclusion in their portfolio. Where there is even the tiniest bit of doubt, it should not be included.

ELEMENT 6 : PLAGIARISM

Within photography circles, passing off and plagiarism are often thought of as one and the same, but they are actually fundamentally different. Plagiarism is not a legal term; the correct name for it is copyright infringement and, whilst passing off is comparable to fraud, plagiarism is comparable to theft! Stealing substantial bits from other's work, copying something from a book or photograph, and basing the image on another's without original re-working or parody, are all examples of plagiarism.

Care should be taken by all photographers when receiving a brief, particularly if it is accompanied by a copy of another photographer's image, or a sketch of an image you think you recognise. If you are told: "I want it to look like that", the alarm bells should start to ring. The resulting image may be a copyright infringement; you may be implicated legally and your reputation will probably not be enhanced by your act. The instructions you are given may not appear to point towards a possible act of plagiarism - it may just be a moral decision on your part. If you feel uneasy, or are at all unsure, speak out! You could be saving yours, and your client's, reputation.

ELEMENT 7 : PHOTOGRAPHER AND CLIENT RELATIONSHIP

The commissioner of a photograph is looking for someone they can trust and with whom they can develop a relationship, which means the photographer and art director often become friends. However, business relationships which depend only on friendship for the terms on which that business is conducted often end in recrimination, because everything is done on a 'handshake' rather than through a written contract. Of course it is important to develop friendships whilst working as a team, but get the business arrangements in writing. Clients have more respect for photographers who deal with the business side efficiently and openly, than they do for those who want to 'sort it out over lunch'.

A photographer's reputation depends on what clients have to say about them to one another, and 'horror' stories get around. A photographer who gets their client arrested for trespass, or passes off someone's work as their own, or who runs two days over on a shoot because he/she was busy having liquid lunches with the art director, is not a photographer who will last long!

ELEMENT 8 : PHOTOGRAPHER AND SUPPLIER

The photographer must also develop good professional relationships with his/her suppliers, for, at the end of the day, it is the services which they provide that the photographer depends on.

The photographer uses a wide range of services including: processing laboratories; printers; film and equipment manufacturers and retailers; stylists; home economists; models and model agencies; set builders; modelmakers and hire studios. The relationship between the photographer and each of these services is based on contract law; the terms of the contract are normally given to the photographer by the supplier. Listed below are some of the most frequent problem areas.

Loss and Damage of Film

Film sometimes gets lost on the way to the laboratory, or gets damaged in processing and, very occasionally, the original film stock can be faulty. The suppliers, that is the courier, the laboratory or printer, and the film manufacturer and retailer, are providing services to the photographer. They have a responsibility to ensure that the service is of a reasonable standard and that goods offered to the photographer are of usable quality. They have a duty of care towards the photographer, but, for obvious reasons, they will try to limit the extent of their liability in cases of loss or damage.

The best solution for the photographer is prevention rather than cure. Film should always be tested before use; valuable film should be delivered personally by the photographer or sent with two separate couriers; batches of film should be split during processing, ensuring that only part of the film is processed at a time.

Of course, such solutions are not always practical or even possible, so the second line of defence is for the photographer to carry insurance for the full value of the shoot (u9:e1h:p77). This can be very expensive but may be the only real guarantee, and, of course, the photographer must be prepared to prove their loss to the insurer. This also avoids the need for the photographer to waste time getting into direct conflict with the supplier as the insurer will deal with this side of things.

The third solution is to push directly for compensation; this may be time consuming and the result unsatisfactory, irrespective of the supplier's liability.

The first problem is that the client may be waiting for the shots and will hold the photographer responsible, irrespective of who is to blame. The second difficulty may be in getting the supplier to accept any form of liability, particularly if their own insurance cover was inadequate or perhaps even non-existent.

Then there is the problem of valuing the lost images. If the photographer is commissioned then it may only be a matter of reshooting, but will it be possible to re-assemble the elements? The photographer may be able to retake the photographs, but will the results be the same? Some things can never be recaptured, for example a goal at a football match or the Berlin Wall coming down.

The supplier will probably say that their liability is limited to the replacement of the film. Such a claim by a supplier of professional film or a professional laboratory is unacceptable. However, if the notice they publish limiting their liability was brought to the attention of the photographer first (and it normally isn't produced until there's trouble), then a court might come down on the side of the supplier.

Unfortunately cases of this kind never come to court in the UK so there are no precedents to go by in valuing these types of losses. In most instances a settlement is reached with the supplier out of court.

Goods in Trust

A 'duty of care' has already been mentioned in relation to laboratories and printers, but hire studios and stylists also have a responsibility for the goods belonging to the photographer or their client, or which have been hired on behalf of the photographer (u9:e1j:p78).

Example A roomset photographer working with a stylist in a hire studio, completes a shoot and the set is broken up. The stylist returns some of the goods personally, leaving the rest of the goods in the loading bay of the hire studio awaiting pick up. A number of items go missing.

Who is responsible? The stylist who was supposed to oversee the safe return of the goods, and whose job includes return of goods? The hire studio who provided the storage space and are responsible for security? The delivery company which was not on site to pick up whilst the stylist was present? Or, of course, the photographer, whose client wants to know why there is now an additional £500 costs on the invoice? Each of those suppliers should carry 'goods in trust' insurance, as should the photographer.

To summarise, the photographer should not entrust film to an unknown supplier. Suppliers should always be professional and the photographer should check their track record. The photographer should always carry insurance where possible

ELEMENT 9 : PHOTOGRAPHER, AGENT AND LIBRARY

The relationship between a photographer and an agent, and a photographer and a library, is somewhat different. Agents exist to find work for photographers. Agencies and libraries market material which already exists or has possibly been shot speculatively, but for library use.

Picture Libraries

It is essential to have a contract with an agency or library. This will ensure both parties know exactly what is expected of them. The British Association of Picture Libraries and Agencies (BAPLA) produces a standard document (*ill 9:p123*) which covers most eventualities, but it must be understood that this is a proper contract and it should not be signed by either side until both are satisfied that it adequately reflects their wishes. Clauses may be altered to suit different circumstances but all such alterations should be carefully discussed before anything is signed to ensure the contract does not become one-sided.

It must be clear from the outset how long the photographer will be required to leave their material with the agency or library and how much notice must be given of intention to terminate the agreement. The contract should indicate who is responsible for insurance and how frequently payments due will be made.

If a relationship with an agency or library turns sour, it is in the interests of both sides that it be terminated as soon as possible, whatever the contract may indicate, but only with the agreement of both parties.

Agents

Whether or not to take on an agent is a decision that most photographers will have to make at some point in their career, specifically if they are working in the advertising or design fields. Those working mainly in the editorial field will generally represent themselves because of the low day rates and the one to one relationships which tend to exist between photographers and editors. Photographers take on agents for the same reasons that they would any other service provider: when the time or skill to do what is required is beyond their reach.

Ideally, the creator is the best person to sell their work. Commissioners are hiring the photographer, not just their work, and a good working relationship is important. Many photographers enjoy selling themselves and their work, accepting rejection as part of the game, whilst others take rejection personally and prefer to leave the selling to an agent. Selling to busy and often distracted people can be frustrating when it is yourself you're selling; some photographers may look at it as a challenge; others will fall at the first hurdle. Agents have generally already made many contacts in the business and know the right people to get in and see, often without having to join the waiting list which many art buyers, through necessity, have to compile.

Tailoring a portfolio to a specific need, and showing it to its best advantage, means being objective; not always an easy thing to do for the creator, but easier for an outside trained eye. Many established agents will gladly help young or more established photographers by viewing their portfolios and advising on its presentation, as well as pointing them to the right agent if required.

Not all agents work in the same way; some work just as representatives, taking the portfolio round the agencies and negotiating jobs; others offer complete accounts packages, dealing with all negotiations, paperwork and invoicing. Some will work on a retainer plus a percentage for each job secured and completed, whilst others will just work on a percentage of the photographer's fee per job.

It's a matter of personal choice as to which option is chosen, but, either way, an agreement must be reached as to monies paid and responsibilities shared. The Association has put together a standard contract (*ill 8:p121*) which can either be used as printed, or as a guideline to show the areas that should be addressed and agreed. Trust, a good working relationship, and a common goal are important factors to take into consideration when considering joining forces with an agent.

SUMMARY

There are a wide range of difficult situations in which the photographer may find themselves; not all are ethical issues, but young photographers should develop a code of practice for themselves. This will give them a standard to which they are prepared to work and will help them guard against the unprofessional behaviour of others.

Unit 5 : Contracts and Licensing

INTRODUCTION

Contracts and licensing combine the most important aspects of both standards of practice and copyright law. This unit provides an understanding of these, to enable photographers to make their legal rights work for them economically, whilst ensuring that all parties' rights are respected.

ELEMENT 1 : BASIC CONTRACT LAW

A contract is a legally binding agreement, ie. an agreement which will be enforced by the courts, and can be made between two or more persons. There must be a meeting of minds upon a common purpose to form an agreement: consensus ad idem (agreement of ideas). Absence of consensus can make a contract null and void, eg. where both parties are genuinely mistaken as to each others' intentions. Each party must be free to consent to the contract without being put under undue duress or being induced fraudulently.

Example A photographer agrees a daily rate based on the client stating that the usage was to be a small run of leaflets; when the work was published it was on billboard posters. The client knew from the outset that the work was to be used on posters, therefore the contract was fraudulently induced.

A contract would not be legal if it involved an illegal act, eg. child pornography.

A contract is usually in the form of a commercial bargain: an offer, an acceptance, and a consideration (payment). The payment does not have to be a tangible amount or even the market value, just "something of value"; for example, in the wake of the 1988 Copyright Act, letters were sent to photographers by commissioning agencies which were copyright assignments and included a £1 coin. Photographers who accepted the £1 coin, accepted the contract and were considered to have lost their copyright to that particular agency. Although ignoring the letter and not returning the coin would not mean that the photographer had agreed to the assignment, returning the coin and the letter, clearly rejecting the agreement, would leave the agency in no doubt about the photographer's position.

Contracts do not have to be in written form, but obviously, should problems arise, something in a tangible form is easier to prove. If a problem arises with a verbal agreement, the onus is on each party to prove what they understood the contract to be. If the parties have worked together on previous jobs then a lot of the argument would rest on what had become "normal practice" between them.

The Association of Photographers actively encourages its members to get as much in writing as is practicably possible and, even if paperwork is not forthcoming from the commissioner, the photographer should confirm, themselves, all aspects of the job in writing.

ELEMENT 2 : PHOTOGRAPHER AND CLIENT

An estimate (*ill 1:p105*) is given to a client and is based on the initial instructions from the client. These instructions are the job offer. The estimate (u3:e9a:p36) forms the basis on which the job is to be confirmed and should always include the terms and conditions on which the photographer will complete the commission. It is important that this first paperwork gives the client an opportunity to see on what conditions they are using the services of the photographer. This is the acceptance of the offer and outlines the terms of the consideration. If the figures are acceptable an order will be sent by the client, or a telephone call will be made by the client accepting the estimate.

ELEMENT 3 : CLIENT AND PHOTOGRAPHER

On acceptance of the estimated figures, an order should be received from the client. This is the acceptance of the terms and completes the first part of the contract. If a written order is not received, but the estimate is accepted by telephone, then the photographer should confirm the conversation in writing by fax and post.

Written orders should be read thoroughly because terms and conditions from the client will normally be on this document and may contradict the original instructions on which the estimate was based. Points to look out for are:

a) Copyright assignment to client (u1:e4:p16)
b) Moral rights waiver (u2:e4:p29)
c) Media use
d) Duration of licence
e) Territory of use
f) Indemnity clause (see opposite)
g) Syndication for editorial work (u5:e8b:p53)

The photographer should notify the client immediately if any of the terms are unacceptable, particularly if they contradict what was originally agreed.

ELEMENT 4 : EQUITABLE ASSIGNMENTS

The 1988 Copyright Designs and Patents Act states that an assignment must be in writing and signed by the copyright owner. Unfortunately this is not the only way that an assignment can be made; many photographers wrongly believe that if they don't sign something, they haven't assigned their copyright.

Example 1 By accepting and working on an order which includes a copyright assignment, the assignment becomes a condition of the contract. With or without your signature the agency owns the copyright in equity.

Example 2 One of the rules of entry into a photographic competition is that copyright of the images entered is assigned to the competition organisers; a signature is not required. By entering the competition, knowing the rules of entry, a legally binding contract is formed and the organisers own your copyright in equity.

Equity is a system which developed over the centuries in order to qualify the rules created by legal precedent. Originally, equity was handed out by a different court from the courts which applied the law. Equity and Law are now dispensed by all the civil courts, but they remain as two different sets of rules. How this applies to the ownership of copyright is thus:

- The law says an assignment of copyright is only effective if it's signed by the copyright owner, but the contract says the client/organiser is entitled to that assignment.
- The copyright is still the photographer's at law, but it's the client/organiser's in equity.
- The photographer is still the legal owner of the copyright, but the client/organiser is the beneficial owner and is treated by equity as having all the rights of the legal owner.
- The photographer is in effect a trustee holding the copyright on behalf of the real owner.

If an order received from a client includes an assignment of copyright clause, and you have not agreed to assign the copyright, it is imperative that you point this out to them. Don't ignore it; by working on it you are accepting the terms of the contract.

ELEMENT 5 : THIRD PARTIES

a) Models
b) Set Builders
c) Model Makers
d) Background/Scenic Artists
e) Stylists
f) Hair and Make-Up Artists
g) Home Economists
h) Location Finders
i) Laboratories
j) Agents
k) Hire Studios
l) Assistants

A photographic shoot may include any or all of the above third parties (anyone involved in the shoot other than the photographer and client/agency - eg. subcontractors used by the photographer) and each will have some form of contract with the photographer; a) to d) may have rights within the image. An indemnity clause in an art order will expect the photographer to indemnify the agency/client against any third party claims. The clause ensures that the client will not be responsible for problems which may arise from the use of anyone, or anything, within the image. This may be a prop, photograph, etc, the copyright of which belongs to another artist, and for which clearance has not been sought, regardless of whether the client insisted the product was to be used, against the advice of the photographer.

Models, or their agencies, license the use of their image in a similar way to photographers, that is they are paid for the exact media, territory and time period the image will be used for. Major exposure of a model's image can deplete their earning potential. A model who has been seen in many magazines or advertising campaigns will be unlikely to be used, for example, by Revlon as a new face. The model agencies are therefore very careful when considering payment for the use of a model. When booking models be sure you are aware of the terms under which you are booking the model; many large agencies put the onus on the photographer to discover if the model has previously worked for clients whose products may be in direct competition with the product you are shooting. Model agencies' terms and conditions are often printed in their Agency Model Book and the booking will refer to these terms.

Example 1 The model has been paid for editorial use and the client uses the shot for advertising. The model has a right to further payment; the photographer could be liable if they booked the model and the order included an indemnity clause.

Example 2 A stylist has supplied an item for the shoot, which is an original and, as such, is the copyright of another artist. The stylist has not sought permission from the copyright owner for the item to be used in an advertising context, although the copyright owner was happy for editorial use. Another artist's copyright has been breached as the item was used in an advertising campaign and the photographer is liable if the indemnity clause is accepted.

If possible the indemnity clause should be removed or changed to ensure liability of the photographer is limited only to those third parties or items the photographer has engaged. Ensure all third parties are aware of the use agreed with the client/agency. Model Release Forms (u3:e9d:p37) or other basic contracts should echo the photographer's licence, and should be copied to all parties so they all know the boundaries.

ELEMENT 6 : TERMS AND CONDITIONS

Terms and conditions of the photographer must accompany all paperwork extended to clients and third parties. All parties must be aware of the grounds on which the contract is being executed. The photographer should be aware that terms on the client's order can override the photographer's terms, as shown on the estimate, and so any differences between the two should be agreed before the shoot begins. The Association of Photographers has produced terms and conditions which have been agreed with agencies as workable and give protection to the photographer, and these are registered with the Office of Fair Trading. These should be included on the reverse of estimate, invoice & licence to use forms (*ills 1:p106, 2:p108, 3:p110*). They are negotiable and if not queried by the client can be deemed as accepted. All the clauses are important, particularly the following:

2. Copyright
3. Ownership of materials
4. Usage
6. Client confidentiality (u4:e4:p43)
7. Indemnity
12. Right to a credit (paternity right) (u2:e2:p27)
14. Electronic storage.

Clause 4 - USAGE - is of particular importance with regard to payment terms, because it affords the photographer protection should the commissioning body cease trading before payment is received, and allows the photographer a chance to claim payment from the ultimate client. It also provides another avenue should payment be late and there are difficulties in being paid; the user is in breach of copyright if the work is being used whilst the photographer's bill remains unpaid. This clause has been successfully used by working photographers.

ELEMENT 7 : LEGALITY AND RETROSPECTIVE ORDERS

Written contracts do not have to be signed to make them legally binding; accepting and working on a contract, or order, can be deemed as acceptance. Emphasis must be put on reading all paperwork and acting immediately, in writing, on any parts that are not acceptable to the photographer, or are different to the original discussions on which the estimate was based.

Art orders received during, or after, the shoot are "in retrospect" and are not legally binding. As stated before, each party has to know the terms they are working on before commencement. Estimates are based on the information given, concerning territory, media, time periods, exclusivity and the photographer retaining copyright. Orders received after or during the shoot which negate any of these areas do not form part of the contract and should be returned to the client as unacceptable, stating that the original costs were estimated on the agreed areas of use in the initial conversation. Any agreed changes to these terms naturally affect the costs, which should then be renegotiated. Unfortunately this is sometimes difficult in practice as the Art Director may turn up, on the day of the shoot, with the art order, so photographers should make time to check through it immediately, and inform the client/agency, on the spot, of any problems.

ELEMENT 8 : NEGOTIATING LICENCES (u1:e4:p16)

Advertising

When the photographer is originally approached with a possible commission, great care needs to be taken in assessing the exact needs of the client, because the costing is dependant on this information. Many clients still want to obtain copyright from the photographer for a variety of reasons, the main ones being a lack of 'copyright' understanding and the fear of having to spend more money for further use.

Standard trade practice, with reference to the original commission, will give the client exclusivity for the period of time, in the specific territories agreed, included in the shoot fee. Within advertising this exclusivity extends to four years after the licence has expired, unless otherwise agreed at the time of commission. When the initial exclusivity period has expired, the original commissioner is usually given the option to extend the exclusivity period. The sensitivity of the subject matter should always be taken into consideration, for example, an image which could be used to good effect by a competitor of the original client. NB. A licence is deemed to begin from the date of first insertion, when the campaign begins. Fees for UK or any single EU country are usually based on the following alternatives:

a) 1 year - any two of the following media: Press, poster, POS, Direct Mail, TV, •Brochure, •Packaging, Merchandising ('purchasable or give-away'). A 3rd media may be included depending on its proportion of the media spend.

OR

b) 2 years - any one of the above media.

Fees for initial use outside the EU are normally based on one media for a period of 1 year only.

• These media should have seperate negotiations when requested as an additional media, dependant on print run and 'life span'.

When the original fee is being negotiated, the Base Usage Rate (BUR) should also be established. The BUR is the figure around which all future negotiations for use outside the original licence, or after its expiry, should be based. Payment for re-use of an image will be a percentage of this figure. BUR (*ill 7:p117-120*) is still not used by all agencies and photographers but more are beginning to use it as a means of giving the client an idea of future expenditure.

BUR should not be calculated at less than the photographer's day rate, and is generally a figure between the day rate and the shoot rate (photographer's fee only, not expenses) in the case of shoots of more than one day.

The BUR table (*ill 7:p117-120*) has been written by major advertising agencies together with the Association of Photographers, and is registered with the Office of Fair Trading. It shows how to apply the BUR and gives more detail on usage within advertising. Whilst these figures are advertising based, they can also be looked at as a possible way of negotiating re-usage in other sectors of the industry. It should be borne in mind that advertising media has a major visual impact on a very wide audience and therefore budgets are higher than in other sectors, eg. corporate brochures, which have a smaller viewing and so lower figures should be used. In all areas it should be stressed that all figures within photography are negotiable and the budget restrictions of the client must be taken into consideration, but if it's impossible to do the work well, within the budget, the client should be made to understand this and the commission re-thought.

There will always be times when the client is adamant with regard to purchasing all rights at the outset, and the All Uses Licence was devised to allow the photographer copyright and moral rights whilst affording the client all other rights. All Uses gives the client worldwide, all media, exclusive use of the work, in perpetuity (*ill 7:p118*). It is an expensive exercise for the client, but it means that no further usage fee needs to be paid. All Uses also allows the photographer to retain the copyright, and the moral rights of the work cannot be sold on to another party; it is not an asset of the company should they go into receivership, and it prevents the client altering the work - whether manually or electronically - without permission. A good selling point to the client to have an exclusive licence, as opposed to copyright ownership, is that, as exclusive licence holder, the client takes on most of the rights of the copyright owner and they have the right to sue anybody, including the photographer, for any infringements during the term of the licence.

Editorial

Magazine expectations differ between publications. Many will expect to syndicate the work for six months after the first insertion. Syndication gives the magazine the right to put the work into their own library and re-sell it to other magazines without further permission from the photographer. Payment on a percentage basis is sometimes given to the photographer each time the image is published; the percentage is pre-set and usually not negotiable.
The three main areas of rights requested by magazines and publishing houses are:

i) All Rights, entire world copyright (all photographer's rights to the image are lost).
ii) All Rights with syndication, entire world copyright, with "X" amount paid to the photographer for the first occasion the work is re-published within the publishing group. This is a one time payment only, after the original commission payment.
iii) First British Rights with exclusivity, copyright remains with photographer. The work is published once only, in one magazine, and kept exclusive to the magazine for up to 6 months after the work is completed. Work is returned to the photographer after publication.

It is vital that the photographer is sure of the rights the magazine is purchasing and is aware that editorial rates are extremely low.

One major publishing house - Haymarket - requests signatures, confirming the rights granted, on the back of their cheques before banking. The cheque will arrive with a remittance advice attached to it and on this remittance will be the rights to use the photographs that have been purchased. It is important to check that these rights are the same as those agreed before the work was started. If they are the same as discussed, then a signature on the cheque will just confirm the agreement, and the cheque can be banked. If they differ, then signing and banking the cheque will give the magazine the rights they want, not the rights they discussed. For example, if first British Rights were agreed, the advice may say 'All Rights'. Telephone the contact at the magazine, explain the problem and request a new cheque. Altering the cheque, or not signing where indicated before banking it, may result in the cheque being returned unpaid. Some Publishing Houses have got wise to the fact that photographers were changing the wording and signing the cheque anywhere but on the dotted line, and have instructed their banks not to pay these cheques. Remember, if the correct terms and conditions have been used, the magazine will be in breach of copyright if they use the work before the photographer is paid!

IPC and Southbank Publishing were once the leaders in the 'cheque signing practice'. Since they consulted a leading copyright lawyer in the early eighties, this practice has become their standard procedure. At the time of writing we understand that this practice is being phased out and, after an unsuccessful attempt to secure a blanket assignment from all contributors, been replaced by a 'multiple choice' system.

Dependant on the commissioning magazine's stance on photography there appears to be four different methods of acquiring rights:

1) Assignment of 'All rights' for the commission in hand.
2) Blanket assignment of 'All Rights' for all future commissions.
3) First publication right, photographer retains copyright but pays expenses incurred on shoot.
4) 'Qualified Rights' to cover all future commissions
   - first right to reproduce in commissioning magazine
   - unlimited re-use relating to commissioning magazine
   - unlimited re-use in all IPC & affiliated publications, 40% royalty fee per use
   - worldwide syndication in perpetuity, 40% royalty fee per use
   - photographer retains copyright

In any large publishing house each magazine editor has their own way of commissioning, and determining what rights they will buy. Many magazines will automatically go for the blanket 'All Rights' option, with a view to cutting down on future paperwork, but they may also be willing to negotiate on a 'job by job' basis. 'Photographer paying own expenses' may not be the case with many editors, who would be happy to pay the normal day rate plus expenses for one time use only. 'Qualified Rights' may not have to mean that work is syndicated by IPC in perpetuity, but can be returned to you after a negotiated period.

Don't take what is first offered as being the only option. The fact that the various options are available, within the magazine group, gives you more scope for negotiation. Editorial rates are still amongst the lowest in the industry; being able to re-sell the work yourself, or through your stock library, can make editorial work a more viable prospect. The Association of Photographers strongly advises against taking either of the 'all rights' options.

The Internet has become the new plaything of the Publishing world, giving the magazines yet another excuse to insist they own copyright in the image. Conde Nast, IPC, Reed and BBC Worldwide publications already have some of their titles on the Net, and some are looking at becoming interactive in the very near future. The Internet should be treated, for licensing purposes, as just another media; there is no need for an assignment of copyright, a licence will suffice (u12:e4:p100). When work is commissioned, or submitted, discuss with your magazine contact the possibility of them wanting to publish on the Net. Try to agree a price, or if you are happy for them to use the image without payment, make sure you are credited either alongside the image or on the lead page. If you decide not to charge, put a time period on the deal when you will re-discuss the merits of the Net and whether it has been a profitable venture for both yourself and the magazine. Use of your image on the Internet, without your permission, is a breach of copyright - the same as any other media.

Magazine contracts to secure all rights - 'past, present, and future throughout the universe in any and all forms of media now in existence or hereafter developed' - have been doing the rounds for the past 2 years. These contracts are a way of ensuring that all commissioned work will be available, payment free, for any electronic transmission or computer storage (eg. CD-ROM). Do not feel duty bound to accept these onerous contracts to ensure you work for the magazine again! Many photographers have refused to sign and negotiated better deals. Talk to the magazine's contact and explain what YOU want to sell them. The Association of Photographers has been in talks with many of the major publishing houses. If you are in doubt, talk to other photographers working in your field and call The Association if you feel you are fighting a 'lone battle'.

SUMMARY

Contracts are entered into every day by people in all walks of life; negotiating the purchase or lease of any item becomes contractual, for example, purchasing a train or bus ticket enters you into a contract. Most everyday contracts are oral, but where something as important as a person's livelihood is concerned, the terms should be in writing. Peoples' minds fog; what one person understands as one thing, another person can interpret as something totally different. Write them down, agree them in writing, and when time is short use the fax, because confusion can be very frustrating. Terms and conditions of business are used by everybody and photographers should not have to accept other people's terms whilst not being able to impose their own. Contracts serve to protect both parties and their proper use should not embarass or impede either party.

Unit 6 : Europe

INTRODUCTION

The aim of this unit is to provide an introduction to some of the issues of interest to photographers who wish to work in other parts of Europe. The key points covered in this unit are:

- Harmonisation of standards and legislation, particularly in the area of copyright law, which affect every aspect of the photographer's business and working practice.
- Working in several marketplaces at once.
- New creative influences.

ELEMENT 1 : WHAT HARMONISATION MEANS FOR PHOTOGRAPHERS

What is the European Union?

The European Union (EU) is a group of 15 nations which have joined together to form an economic and social grouping able to trade without tariffs (cross border taxes), without sanctions (political blocks) and without bureaucratic or legal restrictions. The job of the EU is to see that none of these stop the free movement of goods or services across the Union and to investigate, and if deemed necessary recommend, legislation which facilitates free trade to the European Parliament.

The European Union should also mean that the small countries of Europe, by working together as part of a powerful union, have equal weight in the global market, for instance when negotiating with the trade blocks of America and Japan.

What is Harmonisation?

The original aim of EU harmonisation policy was to draw the social, economic and legal systems of each of the countries within the Union together, so that ultimately those systems would be the same across the Union. Such a goal is difficult to achieve and is one of the reasons for complaints about the size of the bureaucracy (European Commission) which runs the Union. Following the Maastricht Treaty, when nations such as the UK and Denmark dissented from this policy of unification, the harmonisation programme was changed and the term 'subsidiarity' became the watchword. From this point, laws will only be made to rectify situations which stop or hinder the freedom of trade within the Union, and the job of the Commission is to put this policy in place.

The Commission of the European Community is made up of different directorates, each of which is responsible for harmonisation in its area of responsibility. Copyright, for example, is part of Intellectual Property which is covered by Directorate General XV (DG15) and New Technologies come under DG13.

How do Photographers have a say in Harmonisation?

The directorate which has a general responsibility for a particular area, will normally look at the issues which they feel need harmonisation and decide on the order in which these issues are to be investigated. Normally a consultation paper, for example on 'moral rights', is produced and circulated to interested parties. These may be national groups including trade associations such as the Association of Photographers; interest groups such as the British Copyright Council; or European groups such as Pyramide (which is constituted as a European Economic Interest Group to represent the interest of photographers, illustrators and designers). Professional associations should have some form of involvement with each kind of group, so that their voice, and those of their members, are heard in a variety of ways. In the case of copyright, other interested groups such as those representing publishers, producers, users and consumers, also take part. All these groups are then asked to respond to a questionnaire on the subject and normally a hearing is organised as a follow-up to the questionnaire. At the hearing the many interest groups are given an opportunity to make their case and to debate the issues involved.

In the case of 'moral rights', those interest groups representing the users of copyright (eg. publishers and advertisers) were strongly against harmonisation, and the creators (eg. photographers and artists) were strongly in favour. The 'users' argued that moral rights cause problems for publishers, and the 'creators' argued that individual creators need a single unified law for practical reasons and that creators in certain European countries were operating at a disadvantage to others. National governments, both within and outside the Union, along with international organisations such as WIPO (World Intellectual Property Organisation) also had an opportunity to put their views forward.

The Commission then considered the arguments which formed part of a final recommendation as to whether legislation is needed. In the case of 'moral rights' the decision was to defer any further action.

If legislation is recommended, it normally takes the form of a draft Directive on which there are further consultation opportunities. Once in its final form, the Directive is put before the European Parliament, where MEPs (Members of European Parliament) can be lobbied for further amendments. Once adopted the Directive must also be adopted and implemented in the national legislation of each member State of the European Union. There are further opportunities for consultation and some slight amendments made at national implementation level.

Pyramide

Pyramide was founded and took its name from a meeting held in the Pyramide of The Louvre in 1989, when the founding members signed a declaration of ten items (the Manifesto of the Pyramide) of fundamental legislative importance to photographers.

Pyramide has its European Headquarters in Brussels and each nation or national group has its own Pyramide, which in turn is a member of the European organisation. Within Europe and the USA, Pyramide currently represents over 75,000 creators.

The sole purpose of Pyramide is bounded by the points of the Manifesto. These are the ten articles of the Manifesto of the Pyramide:

Article 1	The Photographer is invested, by reason of the creation of his work, with unassailable moral rights and its copyright.
Article 2	The moral rights are rights personal to the Author and relate to his name, work and his status as a creator and to the manner in which his work is reproduced and to his right to withhold any rights of reproduction.
Article 3	The 'Patrimonial Right' is the exclusive right of the Photographer during his life to exploit his work in such a manner as he wishes and to receive profit from this.
Article 4	a) The Photographer is paid for the work he carries out and is also paid for the right to use. b) Fees paid relate to the creation and production of the photograph. c) Any use of the photograph requires the prior written agreement of the Photographer on the use of the photograph and a payment for the right to use from the client. d) Permission for the use of the photograph and the validity of the written agreement from the Photographer concerning the transfer of usage rights depends on the precise terms of the agreement and related specified fees for each usage based on the geographical area, the term, the importance of the image and the type and context of use. e) Any use of the photograph, total or partial, without the written consent of the Photographer or which exceeds the agreed scope of use is an infringement.
Article 5	Each user of the photograph must, even in the absence of a contract, declare usage of the photograph to the Photographer. Each user of the photograph must send, free of charge, two evidential copies of the photograph to the Photographer at least one of which must be a complete copy. If these copies are not sent, two evidential copies of usage must be put aside for the use of the Photographer without him having to claim them.
Article 6	The Photographer retains ownership of the photographic work and any supporting material delivered to the client. When the agreed usage period expires all the photographic materials entrusted for this period must be returned to the Photographer in the condition in which they were delivered originally.
Article 7	Any reproduction or use of the photograph, in the absence of a waiver of

	moral rights, must give a credit of the name and status of the Photographer beneath or next to the photograph.
Article 8	It is the Photographer alone who is responsible for the selection and choice of his image given for usage. Any change or modification to the photograph (eg. montage, changing of the image, photographic distortion, colouring or digital storing of the image) is not permitted except with the consent of the Photographer.
Article 9	In the event that any photograph, transparency or duplicate is lost, damaged or is not returned the client must compensate the Photographer for the loss he has suffered or for the agreed value if this had been specified in the contract.
Article 10	Any input, manipulation or transmission of the photographic image by any digital or electronic system requires the prior consent of the Photographer in writing concerning the terms under which the photograph may be inputted, used or transmitted.

Since the original meeting, Pyramide Europe now encompasses a total of 10 countries, with Sweden & the USA as observer members. The Association of Photographers is the headquarters for Pyramide UK & Ireland.

Key Areas of Policy which Affect Photographers

At present the main areas are:

- Intellectual Property (Copyright)
- Harmonisation of Qualifications
- Registration of the Professions
- New Technology

Photographers are also affected indirectly by Competition Policy, Cultural Policy, and directorates responsible for Health and Safety and Employment. Photographers should also look for opportunities for funding which are available through a variety of European initiatives.

ELEMENT 2 : COPYRIGHT

There are fundamental differences between the British view of copyright and the view of much of the rest of Europe (u1:e1:p11). In practice this manifests itself in the way in which creators are protected, the recourse they have against copyright infringement and the stronger position held by creators outside the UK.

Nevertheless, any photographer entering into a contract with an overseas client should try to ensure that the contract is made under British law (English, Welsh or Scottish), not because British law is the best, but because familiarity with British law makes it easier for the photographer and their advisers to negotiate terms and to enforce the law if needed. The fact that there are still many separate legal jurisdictions within the Union makes it very difficult for a photographer, as a sole trader, to operate. Relying on a law with which the photographer is not familiar may cause problems, not least being the financial costs of pursuing any case.

The process of rationalisation of copyright legislation has begun, for example, the UK has now adopted the directive on Duration of Copyright (u1:e2g:p14), and there are other areas such as Rental and Lending, Cable and Satellite, and Information Society where action is imminent.

ELEMENT 3 : WORKING PRACTICE

Perhaps more important than law is a knowledge of working practice in the country or countries where the photographer chooses to operate. This knowledge is not available in books; it can only be acquired through experience and personal research.

Of course, The Association of Photographers publishes its own Standards of Practice for Advertising Photographers (see Unit 3), but even these mean little until the photographer is actually operating as an advertising photographer. Similar publications will be available from professional organisations in other parts of Europe, but will first need to be translated and then discussed with a practitioner working in that field, in that country.

Photographers should be aware that, in some countries of Europe, it is necessary for the individual to register as a professional photographer before setting up in business. Registration takes very different forms in each country. In some it is no more than token registration with the police, but in others it is a matter of studying and taking examinations, both theoretical and practical; being sponsored by another photographer; or by becoming a member of a recognised trade or professional organisation. For an established freelance photographer, perhaps based in the UK but working across borders, it is more a matter of supply and demand.

ELEMENT 4 : WORKING IN OTHER PARTS OF EUROPE

Most British photographers will choose to maintain a permanent business and client base in their country of origin, that is the UK, but will hope in time to receive commissions from clients operating in other parts of Europe.

In this case, the greatest difficulty they face is getting their work known in those other countries. Perhaps the easiest way to achieve this is to build a reputation in the UK which will encourage demand from clients in other parts of Europe. This reputation can be enhanced by advertising, a European tour with a portfolio, an exhibition, or by working with an agent. It is probably true to say that any agent operating elsewhere in Europe, or across Europe, will only be interested in representing a photographer who is successful in their home marketplace and who already has a portfolio of work for prestigious clients.

There is a great deal of respect for British photography, particularly advertising photography, in other European countries, and the UK is in fact regarded as a centre for photography. Many successful British based photographers make a reasonable percentage of their income from overseas clients. It is easier to achieve this if the photographer first makes a reputation for themselves in their home market.

It is possible to take advertisements in some of the many reference books and creative magazines which are published in every country in Europe, but research is needed first to find out which are read by potential clients. There is still no single European source book and the cost of advertising in a number of different publications will be high. Advertisements need support from an agent who will keep the portfolio circulating constantly and who will provide local back up for the photographer.

Styles and aesthetics differ widely between the countries of Europe and, whilst one style of photography may appeal to French taste, it may not appeal to Belgian taste. A large number of photography festivals are held annually around Europe, and not just for exhibition purposes. They include discussions and debates, open sessions for portfolios, and provide publishing opportunities and competitions. It is well worth attending such events and getting involved, firstly for enjoyment, but also to make contacts, to learn something about attitudes to photography, and to get reactions to your portfolio.

Europe is now a single market to be explored and enjoyed for its opportunities.

SUMMARY

Photographers must decide on what level they want to be involved and work in other countries within Europe before they can acquire the additional skills and knowledge which they need to work in this broader marketplace. Clearly, those with language skills can, if they choose, take advantage of this at an early stage, but for the young photographer generally, such decisions are made as part of the natural progression of their career. The rest of Europe, and indeed the rest of the world, has always been open to the successful photographer. The best chance of success for the photographer in the wider market is to acquire language skills and to have a willingness to learn from and participate in other cultures.

Whether or not the photographer chooses to work outside the UK, they should be aware that the UK is now part of Europe, and that decisions made and practices adopted across Europe will affect everyday life in the UK. It is more important than ever that photographers are represented in this process, and that they take an interest in developments in technology, law, trade practice and culture, which the breaching of boundaries will bring.

Unit 7 : Tax and National Insurance

INTRODUCTION

It is essential that any person in any industry should pay both Income Tax and National Insurance contributions on their earnings, as necessary. Therefore, photographers should have an understanding of the differences in status between self-employed and employed personnel, and be aware of their legal obligations of notification and registration with the Inland Revenue and the DSS Contributions Agency. This unit will enable photographers to:

a) ensure they are legally self-employed or an employee and that they are paying appropriate Income Tax and National Insurance Contributions;
b) contact the Inland Revenue and the Contributions Agency at the right time and by appropriate means;
c) keep accurate and up-to-date business records and paperwork;
d) understand the financial responsibilities of the self-employed;
e) understand what expenses are eligible for tax relief for the self-employed.

ELEMENT 1 : INCOME TAX: SELF-EMPLOYMENT (SCHEDULE D) AND EMPLOYMENT (PAYE, SCHEDULE E)

Your employment status affects the Income Tax and National Insurance (NI) contributions you have to pay. It is your responsibility to ensure that you are registered under the appropriate status. The law doesn't define employment but these guidelines help:

Self-Employed Persons

- ultimately decide the course of their business;
- determine their own hours of work;
- have more than one client;
- issue their client with an invoice for which they receive a fee;
- have no contract of employment;
- receive no holiday or sickness pay;
- have to correct unsatisfactory work in their own time and at their own expense, ie. they bear the risks of their own business;
- provide their own tools or equipment.

Employed Persons

- ultimate responsibility for the work is taken by someone else (the employer);
- have regular hours of work;
- work for one company or individual;
- receive a weekly or monthly wage (sometimes calculated hourly) and are eligible for overtime;
- work a standard number of hours per week or days per month and are eligible for overtime in excess of this;
- have a contract or letter of employment;
- are entitled to holiday pay and sickness pay.

Only a small minority of photographic assistants and photographers in fashion, advertising and editorial photography are employed. They receive a regular salary and tax and NI contributions are deducted from their wages before they are received. Employers also pay employer's NI contributions on the wages earned by the employee as part of the Pay As You Earn (PAYE) system.

The majority of the industry works on a freelance basis and is self-employed. A fee, rather than a regular wage, is received in return for providing a service and submitting an invoice. Freelancers are registered with the Inland Revenue as self-employed and have a Schedule D tax reference number.

ELEMENT 2 : SELF-EMPLOYMENT - NOTIFYING THE INLAND REVENUE

It is possible to earn up to £3765 (for the tax year 1996-97) before tax is deducted from an income, but photographers should notify the Inland Revenue as soon as they start freelancing in order to inform them that they are a 'self-employed commercial photographer'. Accurate and up to date accounts for the business should be kept from the start to show:

- the cash status - ie. is there enough to live on?;
- whether the business is making a profit;
- what is owed to the business by clients;
- what is owed to creditors by the business.

Careful and constant attention will mean that accounts are easily managed, either by the photographer or a bookkeeper/accountant, and that problems are easily resolved before any avoidable debt is incurred. Good bookkeeping also ensures that appropriate tax and NI contributions are paid and that it is possible to budget accordingly.

To register as Self Employed, obtain booklet CWL1 "Starting your own business" from your local tax office (tax offices are listed in the telephone directory under 'Inland Revenue'). Complete form CWF 1 (*ill 11:p127*) Notification of Self-Employment (formerly 41G), which can be found in the booklet, and keep a photocopy. Under section 2 enter the nature of the business as 'Commercial Photography'. If you have previously been employed during that year (even vacation work), you will need to include sections 2 and 3 of your P45 (*ill 10:p125*) form. A P45 is a statement of earnings and tax from the previous employment. The CWF 1 form should be sent to the Contributions Agency (see page 65) who will forward a copy to the Inland Revenue. A Schedule 'D' number will be issued, usually within 6 weeks, and this should be quoted on every invoice issued as a photographic assistant, although it is not necessary for a photographer to include the Schedule 'D' reference number on an invoice.

Consider the difference between the tax and NI contributions on the earnings of an employee and a freelancer who earns £10,000 per annum (gross), with travelling expenses of say £1,000 and other expenses of say £1,100:

1996-97	*Tax*	*NI*	*Total Deductions*
Employee (PAYE, Schedule E)	£1340	£748 (Class 1)	£2088
Self-Employed (Schedule D)	£898*	£315 (Class 2)	£1213

These figures are based on a single person's allowance
** includes Class 4 NI collected via Income Tax payments (u7:e6:p67).*

ELEMENT 3 : ACCOUNTS AND BOOKKEEPING

This information is aimed at individuals and partnerships and is not relevant to companies.

Employees' income tax and NI contributions are deducted from pay at source. At the end of the financial year each employee receives a P60 form which summarises these contributions for the financial year. This document is important and should be filed safely because duplicates are not available.

Self-employed people receive fees from which no deductions have been made and should prepare their accounts at least once a year for calculation of their profit/loss, NI contributions and tax assessment. If turnover (fees and expenses) is less than £15,000 per year, there is a system which requires only a summary of business profits rather than the detailed accounts necessary for higher earners. However, this system is ultimately simpler only for the Tax Inspector rather than the Tax Payer because all the necessary details must be kept and organised in order to arrive at the final summary.

The tax year runs from 6th April to 5th April in the following year and is referred to by the years it covers (ie. 6th April 1996 to 5th April 1997 is income tax year 1996-7). The 30th April is the most frequently chosen year end for accounts because of tax sorting and tax postponement benefits for growing businesses. With the new tax system of Self Assessment (u7:e7:p68) we will probably see a change whereby the most frequently chosen year end becomes March 31st. An assessment is based on the profits of the 12 months trading accounts ending in the year of assessment.

In order to keep accurate account of all income and expenditure, self-employed people should ensure that all receipts and bills are kept and organised into months (separate envelopes are sufficient). Cheque payments should be kept separate from payments by cash and credit cards. Details should always be kept on cheque stubs and bank paying-in book counterfoils of dates, amounts and details (eg. what job?) and bank statements for both private and business accounts should be kept in order.

Invoices for freelance work should be submitted from a standard copy invoice book or printed separately and copies filed in order. It is necessary to keep a record of, and to distinguish between, funds used for private expenditure and those drawn from and paid into the business. The following is essential for compiling accurate accounts and balance sheets:

- fees;
- weekly or monthly living expenses taken from the business;
- amounts of clients' outstanding invoices at the accounting year end;
- amounts owed to suppliers (labs and hire companies etc.) and creditors at the year end;
- other money into the business, eg. matured insurance policies, savings, gifts and investments;
- equipment bought and sold for the business (see below);
- running costs of the business.

An example spreadsheet for use either by photographers who have computers with a simple spreadsheet package, or by photographers using a hand written cash book (record of bank account) can be found on pages 139 and 141 (*ills 16 & 17*).

Simple Tax Accounts - for Earnings up to £15,000

Full accounts or a simple summary should be prepared from the date the business started, to either the following 5th April or the date which is 12 months after the date on which the business started. Whatever date is chosen should be kept in future years for convenience.

The summary required for earnings up to £15,000 is relatively simple to complete, providing a good record has been kept of all revenue and expenditure over the 12 month period. An accountant will complete the relevant section from the Self Assessment Tax Return Form, to be submitted to the Inland Revenue as a summary of profits for 12 months. The simple account section requires information concerning only:

	Total Business Earnings (Turnover)	A
Less	Business Expenses and Purchases	B
	Net Profit	C

Line A - Total Business Earnings (Turnover)

Turnover is the gross amount earned by a business before any business expenses are deducted and can be calculated by the total of the invoices submitted in a year. Turnover also includes:

- all money received for cash jobs;
- the value of goods or services received in exchange for work done or goods sold.

(Enterprise Allowance is taxable but should not be included in business turnover. It should be entered on your tax return under the heading 'Trade, Profession, or Vocation'.)

Line B - Business Expenses and Purchases

These are divided between revenue and capital items.

Employees pay tax on all earnings (gross) which is deducted from wages before they are received (net).

Self-employed people pay tax on any earnings over £3765 (1996-97) per annum after the deduction of business expenses, such as travel, film and processing, depreciation of vehicles, telephones, subscriptions and renewal costs.

Accurate records of revenue and expenditure will ensure that money used for living expenses and costs for, and investments in, the business are accounted for. Business costs and investments are usually one of two categories: capital and revenue items.

Capital items are things or investments that are bought and are intended to last for at least a few years, such as cars, equipment and leases. These are claimed in the accounts as 'Capital Allowances'. The present rate for claim is 25% per annum of the written down value each year.

Revenue items are everything else purchased by the photographer, except for items bought for private/non-business use. However, some expenses should be split between business and private use on a percentage basis, such as telephone and motor expenses. There are a couple of grey areas concerning Capital and Revenue Expenditure:

- Small capital items (costing under £100) are sometimes initially classed as Capital Expenditure;
- Large replacements of existing equipment may be treated as Capital Expenditure.

An accountant will help to convince the Inspector of Taxes that both these cases should be treated as Revenue Expenditure.

Line C - Net Profit
Net profit is calculated by deducting the business expenses from the turnover. Tax assessments are based on this final figure and apply to the profits of the accounting year which ends in the tax year, ie. if the tax year of a business ends on the 30th September each year, the 1997-8 assessment is based on profits for the accounting year to 30th September 1997.

Operating Account

Operating account for the year ended 30th April 1996 (example for a typical successful commercial photographer)

	£	£
Income		333,900
Expenses		
Studio Hire	9,197	
Agent's Commission	24,106	
Film & Processing	46,203	
Carriage & Couriers	4,829	
Equipment Hire	4,541	
Props & Set Building	32,721	
Models	11,828	
Location Expenses	237	
Studio Expenses	2,696	
Studio Rent, Rates & Services	8,573	
Studio Light & Heat	1,268	
Assistants & Stylists	30,447	
Motor Expenses (Less 15% Personal Use)	8,262	
Travel Expenses	756	
Overseas Travel & Location Expenses	5,742	
Phone (Less 30% Personal Use of Home Phone) & Fax	2,271	
Printing, Postage & Stationery	1,338	
Subscriptions & Publications	5,920	
Advertising & Publicity	5,920	
Insurance	2,089	
Bookkeeping	698	
Accountancy	2,245	
Bank Charges & Interest	313	
Sundries	65	
Bad Debts (Specific)	61	
Repairs & Renewals of Equipment	2,971	
		215,297
Net Profit for the year		118,603

Balance Sheet

For the year ended 30th April 1996 (a typical successful commercial photographer)

Capital	£	£
Capital brought forward	118,351	
Add: Net Profit for the year	118,603	
	236,954	
Deduct: Drawings	84,809	
		152,145
		152,145
Represented by:		
Fixed Assets		
Motor Vehicles at cost at 1st May 1995	36,948	
Equipment at cost	26,327	
		63,275
Current Assets		
Debtors	80,405	
Cash at Bank	87,768	
	168,173	
Current Liabilities		
Creditors	79,303	
		88,870
		152,145

Note: the balance sheet is like a snap shot of the financial state of the business at its accounting year end.

Depreciation/Capital Allowances

Depreciation of fixed assets is often not shown as an expense in the profit and loss account of sole traders. The Inland Revenue do not allow depreciation as a chargeable expense in the accounts. However, what they do allow is called Capital Allowances. These are allowances of 25% of the written down value of assets each year. These capital allowances are normally shown in the photographer's tax computations which are sent by his/her accountant to the Inland Revenue with his/her accounts. The other advantage of not showing depreciation is that the trading account shows a larger profit, and this can be useful when accounts need to be shown to bank managers and building societies to borrow money or obtain mortgages.

ELEMENT 4 : CONTACTING THE DSS CONTRIBUTIONS AGENCY

Complete form CWF1 (*ill 11:p127*) 'Notification of Self-Employment' (formerly CF11) - see also page 62, registering as Self Employed with the Inland Revenue - and be prepared to quote your National Insurance number. Be aware that employees already paying Class 1 NI contributions on earnings who are also self-employed in another business, are liable to pay Class 1 and 2 NI contributions and also Class 4 if they earn over the lower earnings limit, up to a maximum of Class 1 on its own.

National Insurance Classes

All wage earners must pay National Insurance (NI) contributions which are handled by the Department of Social Security's Contributions Agency. NI contributions support national social security benefits and pensions and are compulsory payments on most earnings.

Local Contributions Agency offices are listed in the telephone directory and the relevant office is determined by your postcode. Write to the appropriate office to register as self-employed, and quote your National Insurance number. There are 4 classes of NI contributions:

Class 1	Paid by employees (PAYE) and collected by the Inland Revenue.
Class 2	Paid by self-employed. Weekly flat rate contributions collected by the Contributions Agency either by direct debit from the bank or Giro account or by quarterly bill.
Class 3	Self-employed and employed. A voluntary contribution of £5.95 per week for low wage earners to protect rights to future benefits and collected by the Contributions Agency. However, it is only approximately 10p per week less than Class 2 contributions and it provides fewer benefits for the self-employed.
Class 4	Self-employed. These are earnings-related contributions on profits between certain limits in a tax year. These are calculated, assessed and collected by the Inland Revenue with Schedule D Income Tax on business profits and are shown on tax assessment forms (tax bills). They yield no benefits.

National Insurance Number

A National Insurance number is issued shortly before your sixteenth birthday. It is made up of two letters, followed by six figures and a single letter. This is a unique reference number which should be used whenever referring to the DSS and which will remain the same all your working life.

Example ZY 65 43 21 X

A National Insurance number is not a Tax Schedule D reference number, which may vary periodically.

ELEMENT 5 : SELF-EMPLOYMENT - CLASS 1 NATIONAL INSURANCE CONTRIBUTIONS ON SCHEDULE D EARNINGS

Some clients require freelance subcontractors to pay Class 1 contributions as employees, although their earnings are usually assessed for Class 4 contributions. This often happens to photographers who are commissioned to do stills on a movie or a commercial, where they will be working with technicians in a union. However, it is possible to get a refund on some contributions if the combined NI contributions exceed certain limits.

Eligibility for refund on Class 4 contributions
If combined Class 1, Class 2 and Class 4 contributions = £2,152.86 or more in 96/97 tax year.

Eligibility for refund on Class 2 contributions
If Class 1 and Class 2 Contributions = £2,152.86 or more in 96/97 tax year

If this applies to you, your Class 4 contributions should be reduced by either:

applying for deferment of the Class 4 NI contributions before the 6th April by completing form CA72B (*ill 12:p129*) from the Contributions Agency.

or applying for a refund of Class 4 contributions at the end of the year by writing to the Contributions Agency, Deferment Group. A refund can only be made if claimed within 6 years from the end of the year of assessment to which the payment relates.

ELEMENT 6 : SELF-EMPLOYMENT - CLASS 2 AND CLASS 4 NI CONTRIBUTIONS

Class 2 NI Contributions

Class 2 NI contributions are not income related and are, for 96/97, a flat rate of £6.05 per week or £314.60 per annum, providing the net income is above the lower earnings limit. Class 2 contributions will help support any future claim you have towards the following benefits:

- basic Sickness Benefit
- basic Invalidity Benefit
- basic Retirement Pension
- basic Widow's Benefit
- basic Maternity Allowance
- Housing Benefit

They do not count towards:

- Unemployment Benefit
- Industrial Injuries Disabled Benefit
- the earnings-related part of Invalidity Benefit
- the earnings-related part of Retirement Pension
- the earnings-related part of Widow's Benefit

Exception Certificate from Class 2 NI Contributions

It is possible to get a Class 2 exception certificate if the net income is less than £3430 in the tax year ending 5th April 1997 by completing form CF10 (*ill 13:p131*) 'Application for Exception from Liability' in leaflet CA72 'NI Contributions: People With Small Earnings From Self-Employment'.

People who have been self-employed for over one year will be asked for accounts evidence to show that sufficiently little has been earned and that there is eligibility for exception. It is not necessary to send accounts details if you have been self-employed for less than a year and it is estimated that earnings will be low enough to be entitled to NI exception. If earnings then exceed the £3430 limit the regular annual contributions of £314.60 will have to be paid. However, no penalty will be incurred for possessing an exception certificate without entitlement.

When completing the CWF 1 'Notification of Self-Employment' form (*ill 11:p127*) for the first time, applicants should indicate they wish to apply for exception from liability for Class 2 Contributions if it is anticipated that earnings will be below the £3430 limit for the year.

It is also possible to receive a rebate on Class 2 contributions if net income was sufficiently lower than expected. This is a long process and you should contact the Contributions Agency to initiate it. If you feel you may be eligible for Class 2 exception it is worth obtaining a certificate and then paying any necessary contributions should income be higher.

Class 4 NI Contributions

Class 4 contributions are income related and are collected by the Inland Revenue with the annual tax assessment. In 1996/97 they are assessed at 6% of net income between the lower earning limit of £6860 (capital allowance) and the upper limit of £23,660.

Example 1: Net Profit for 96/97 of £14,000 (after capital allowances)

	14000	(net profit)
less	6860	(lower limit for Class 4)
	7140 x 6% = £428.40	(Class 4 'tax')

UNIT 7 : TAX & NATIONAL INSURANCE

Example 2: Net Profit for 96/97 of upper limit of £23,660

	23660	(net profit)
less	6860	(lower limit)
	16800 x 6% = £1008	(maximum possible annual Class 4 'tax')

It is worth considering a comparison of NI contributions paid by a PAYE employee and self-employed person.

Example 3: Earnings of £12,000 per annum

	PAYE Employee (Earnings)*	*Self-Employed (Net Profit)*
Earnings	12,000.00	12,000.00
Class 1 NI	948.00	nil
Class 2 NI	nil	314.60
Class 4 NI	nil	12000 - 6860 x 6% = 308.40
Total NI 96/97	948.00	623.00

* based on a single employee of non-pensionable age and not eligible for a reduced rate.
Tax relief on 50% of Class 4 NI Contributions was calculated as a deduction from total income after the calculation of the total Class 4 contributions prior to 1996/97.

ELEMENT 7 : SELF ASSESSMENT AND THE CURRENT YEAR BASIS OF ACCOUNTING

From 6th April 1996, each UK taxpayer is reponsible for assessing his or her own tax. Because of the PAYE system, most employees will not, in the main, notice any difference in the system. Previously, self employed taxpayers received estimated assessments from the Inland Revenue and, when their accounts were agreed, the Inspector issued amended assessments. From 1996/97 the taxpayer will be responsible for ensuring that his/her tax liabilities are calculated and paid to the Revenue by the due date. If a taxpayer wants the Inland Revenue to calculate the tax liability, they will do so, provided the taxpayer's Return is sent in by 30th September following the year of assessment. However, the onus of assessment is with the tax payer and not with the Inland Revenue.

If a taxpayer is prepared to compute their own liability (or get an accountant to compute it for them) then the Tax Return does not need to be sent in until 31st January following the end of the fiscal year. The proposed new Tax Return is shorter than the present one (8 pages instead of 12) but it comes with an enormous booklet of notes giving details of how the form should be filled in, and up to nine schedules requesting additional information (depending on the relevance of those schedules to the taxpayer concerned).

Unlike the present system, the deadlines will be strictly enforced and penalties and surcharges will be levied if Tax Returns are submitted late, even by a few days. It will be essential that all taxpayers ensure that their accounts are kept fully up to date, so that Returns can be completed with the minimum of problem.

Element 3 explained that, under the old system, an assessment for tax was based on the profits of the twelve months trading accounts ending in the previous year of assessment. This has changed. Businesses are now taxed on trading profits for the accounting period ending in the current year. Tax is charged on all other income in the year it is received. Whilst businesses which started after 5th April 1994 go on to the new basis, businesses which started before the 6th April 1994 will have their profits taxed through transitional arrangements which switch their assessment from previous year to a current year basis. The details of these arrangements are complicated and this is not the place to go into the arrangements in detail.

Many people who have previously struggled through their Tax Returns on their own may feel that under self assessment, they need help. Taxation is a complicated subject and it seems set to become more complicated as the Inland Revenue shifts the burden away from itself and on to taxpayers.

ELEMENT 8 : BUDGET 1995

The main allowances for the 1996/97 tax year are as follows:

i) Tax free allowance £3,765.00 (1995/96: £3,525.00)

ii) Class 4 National Insurance Contributions 6.0%. Tax relief on Class 4 NIC Contributions is abolished (1995/96 Class 4 NIC was 7.3% and 50% of the contributions were allowable against tax).

The overall change will mean that there is a small net gain to most self employed people.

The minimum earnings limit for Class 2 National Insurance for 1996/97 is £3430. The 1996/97 flat rate Class 2 weekly contributions amount is £6.05.

The other main changes for 1996/97 which will have significant effect on self-employed photographers are that the band of income taxed at 20% is from £3,766 to £7,665 (1995/96: £3,526 to £6,725). Basic rate tax is reduced to 24% and applies to incomes between £7,666 and £29,265, after which income is subject to higher rate tax of 40% (in 1995/96 the basic rate of 25% applied to taxable income between £6,726 and £27,825 after which income was subject to higher rate tax of 40%.

SUMMARY

Tax and National Insurance are a part of every worker's life. Employees have the advantage of the employer working out their contributions and payments every week or month; the only way the payments are usually noticed is by their absence from their pay slip!

The self-employed have to give more attention to these payments because it is always their responsibility to ensure that payments are made correctly and on time. There are however, certain compensations and the figures in this Unit illustrate how much less a freelancer can pay, compared to an employee earning the same gross salary.

Tax and National Insurance payments are part of the law and cannot be avoided. Getting an FCA accountant who is familiar with the industry, and who understands what expenses are eligible for tax relief can save money and is preferable to using a friend who is simply good with figures. Some photographers feel they can handle this themselves and that they are able to effectively reason and debate with the Inland Revenue and the Contributions Agency, and so avoid using an accountant; this is not recommended.

If photographers start their careers with the belief that freelancing is a series of odd jobs which the Inland Revenue and the Contributions Agency won't be interested in, the attitude will perpetuate. Promises of sorting all the paperwork "next year when I really start earning" are never realised or create many more problems and much bigger bills than would have originally been the case.

Unit 8 : Value Added Tax (VAT) & Customs & Excise

INTRODUCTION

Value Added Tax is a form of indirect taxation on nearly all transactions, which enables the Government to collect revenue from most individuals without directly taxing their income. It is not a tax on turnover, fees or profits, but a tax on consumer spending, collected by HM Customs & Excise on behalf of the Government, and has nothing to do with the Inland Revenue.

It is important that any person in business should understand how VAT effects their income and expenses, and what the legal requirements are for VAT registration and payment.

This unit will define the differences between voluntary and compulsory VAT registration and will clarify those goods and services that are eligible to charge VAT on, and to claim VAT against.

ELEMENT 1 : WHAT IS VALUE ADDED TAX?

Very few things are not subject to VAT and these are either 'VAT Exempt' or 'Zero-Rated' (eg. books and newspapers, most food and the export of some goods). A full list of all these are available in the VAT Guide 700, Appendix A.

However, for most products and services, VAT is applied to every stage of the supply chain of any transaction, at a current rate of 17.5%. A person sells an item and receives money which includes VAT and, by doing so, they indirectly become a collector of money for the Government, because the difference between what was paid and what is received is collected by the VAT office when making a VAT return.

If registered, any job done by a photographer or an assistant is a taxable supply and, as such, is a VAT output. Goods and services from a VAT registered supplier are VAT inputs. VAT charged to your clients must be paid to Customs & Excise after deducting the VAT charged by your suppliers. A broad equation of how VAT works also demonstrates what VAT is:

	VAT on Sales (Output Tax)
less	VAT on Purchases (Input Tax)
=	If output tax is greater than input tax, the photographer pays the difference to the Customs & Excise.
or	
=	If input tax is greater than the output tax, a refund of the difference is paid to the photographer by Customs & Excise

One important thing to consider is that the ultimate VAT cost is borne only by the end user. Finished goods, irrespective of their nature, go through a number of processes, and at each stage of the supply chain, when goods change hands, VAT is applied. However, businesses are allowed to reclaim any VAT they are charged by other businesses; the total reclaims of VAT on inputs is deducted from the VAT on outputs when making the VAT return on form VAT 100 (*ill 15:p137*).

Example A supplier sells film to a photographer for £100.00 and the supplier invoices the photographer £100 + £17.50 VAT, total £117.50. The photographer then takes a photograph and sells it to a gallery for £150.00, and the invoice is for £150 + £26.25 VAT, total £176.25. The gallery sells the print to a member of the public for £200 + £35.00 VAT, total £235.00.

The supplier sends the £17.50 to the Government, the photographer sends £26.50 less £17.50 to the Government, the gallery sends £35.00 less £26.25 to the Government, but the member of the public is not VAT registered and, therefore, the picture has cost them £235.00 and they have just given £35.00 to the Government in indirect taxation.

Therefore, anyone not registered for VAT effectively becomes an end-user and is not allowed to either charge VAT to other people or to reclaim VAT that has been charged to them.

UNIT 8 : VAT & CUSTOMS & EXCISE

ELEMENT 2 : REGISTRATION FOR VAT

Eligibility

It makes no difference whether the business is a Limited Company, a Partnership, or a Sole Trader - the rules are the same. Businesses do not register for VAT, but the Limited Company, sole proprietor or partners do. Photographers who are resident in the UK but who work for clients abroad, or photographers who are resident abroad but who work for UK clients, may still need to be registered for VAT (the local VAT office is able to give further information) - see element 3.

Compulsory Notification

If a photographer's annual turnover (ie. total invoiced income) exceeds £47,000 in any twelve month period (not in just their financial or calendar year), or if they think their turnover will exceed £47,000 in the next one month, they have no choice but to register, by Law, with the VAT office within a month.

Voluntary Registration

If turnover is less than £47,000 (current figure) in any twelve month period then there is a choice: registration can be delayed until the £47,000 threshold is reached, or a photographer can voluntarily register, irrespective of turnover.

Advantages of being VAT Registered

Most of the products or services purchased by a photographer/assistant are subject to VAT, and not being registered for VAT means that all costs will effectively be 17.5% more expensive because it is not possible to reclaim VAT on any of these inputs (purchases). If film costs £50.00, a non-registered photographer will pay £58.75 and will not be able to claim back the additional expense. Therefore, not being registered eats into the profit potential of a business. In addition, VAT registration can positively affect your business by:

i) giving the impression that the business is better established than may be the case;
ii) enabling clients to recover VAT on the expenses recharged to them;
iii) enabling the reclaim of VAT on equipment purchased.

Disadvantages of being VAT registered

Once registered, all business activities and earnings are subject to VAT, including fees for non-photographic related work. Similarly, VAT has to be charged on any sale classified as 'for business use'.

i) Selling, say, an armchair from home is not subject to VAT, but selling an armchair used as a prop must also include VAT and be recorded as a transaction in the business accounts.
ii) Any clients who are not registered with the VAT office will find a VAT-registered photographer's fees and costs more expensive because they will be unable to reclaim the VAT on the invoice.

In general there are few disadvantages to being VAT registered. However, if turnover is fairly low, an accountant's fees should be considered against the amount it is possible to reclaim, and it may be better to wait until turnover is greater.

VAT Invoices - Invoicing clients for VAT amounts

It is a legal obligation for all VAT registered traders to have their VAT number shown clearly on their sales invoices. In addition, VAT at the appropriate rate must be shown as a separate item and the rate (currently 17.5%) on non zero rated sales must be shown. Invoices must be in strict sequence with no gaps, otherwise the suspicions of Customs and Excise will be aroused when a VAT inspection occurs. Cancelled invoices should be kept, as should credit notes.

How to Register for VAT

Contact the local VAT office listed under either 'Customs & Excise' or 'VAT' in the phone directory and ask for Form VAT 1 (*ill 14:p133-136*) and the accompanying booklet. It is also useful to contact an accountant before contacting Customs & Excise.

The date chosen to register for VAT is very important and late payment is liable to fines and penalties. Therefore, if the £47,000 threshold is passed in 12 months, or less, the photographer should register within 30 days of the end of the month in which the threshold was exceeded. The date registration begins is the 1st day of the 2nd month after the end of the month the threshold was exceeded. Unbelievably complicated, but very important.

Threshold Exceeded Month Ending:	*Registration From:*
30th June	1st August
31st March	1st May

It is possible to choose between monthly or quarterly, and recently annual, VAT returns when registering. Monthly returns are really only of benefit if a photographer always has more inputs (purchases) than outputs (sales), and they will therefore always be owed money by Customs & Excise.

It is often simpler if the VAT return date matches the business's financial year, so that the annual turnover and VAT account can be checked simultaneously. Once registered, certain rules must always be adhered to:

i) the VAT registration number should be included on all tax invoices;

ii) invoices should always list the goods and services costs exclusive of VAT. The VAT should then be stated separately and included in the final total;

iii) proper records of transactions need to be kept and submitted on form VAT 100 (*ill 15:p137*). Records should be kept for a six year period and are subject to inspection by Customs & Excise.

ELEMENT 3 : VAT AND TRADING ABROAD/EXPORT OF PHOTOGRAPHY

Some confusion exists concerning VAT and the export of photography abroad, whether it is advertising or editorial work, or whether it is shot in, or produced for a client, in other EU countries or worldwide.

However, the VAT office has been satisfied on a number of occasions that exports of photographic services almost invariably consist of the supply or assignment of copyright and/or licences to use photographs. The VAT Act - 1983, 3 Schedule (Section 7) 1, states that 'Transfers and assignments of copyright, patents, licences, trademarks and similar rights' are all treated as 'supplied where received'. Therefore, VAT is not applied to invoices for work either shot abroad or for a foreign business client, even if shot in the UK.

Sales to the EU can cause potential VAT problems. You can only zero rate your supplies if your customer is VAT registered in their own country. In these cases, their VAT number should be quoted on your invoice. You should speak to your accountant before you invoice your first EU customer.

ELEMENT 4 : ACCOUNTING AND RECORD KEEPING

A person registered for VAT whose turnover is below £350,000 per annum excluding VAT, may, if they wish, account for and pay VAT on the basis of money paid and received, rather than invoices issued and received but not paid. This is known as cash accounting. The main advantage of the scheme is that it defers the time for payment of the VAT where extended credit is given or where clients are slow in paying. However, this system does add some complications to a simple bookkeeping system.

Customs and Excise are very strict in the administration of VAT and it is essential that all VAT registered traders maintain their bookkeeping records meticulously. If a VAT return is sent in late, or VAT is underpaid, there is a system of financial penalties. Most VAT registered people receive a VAT inspection of their records by Customs and Excise within a year or so of first becoming registered. They are then subject to further random inspections every few years.

SUMMARY

If dealt with at the right time and if always kept up to date, VAT should be fairly simple to handle. If matters look a little more difficult, the VAT office is able to give free advice over the phone. When first dealing with VAT it is easy to become distracted by matters that unnecessarily complicate what is sufficient to know. Therefore, photographers should only be concerned with their own activities and know when they should charge VAT or reclaim the VAT that they have been charged by others.

Keeping accurate records is essential for any successful business, but no more so than to monitor progress for tax and financial reasons. Regularly maintaining books, every month, will create fewer problems with VAT, Income Tax, NI Contributions and end of year figures. These are all interlinked and most accounting systems are very simple to use, irrespective of whether they are computerised or manual. The most difficult thing is the discipline required to do the work on a regular basis.

Unit 9 : Insurance & Liabilities

INTRODUCTION

When starting as a photographer or photographic assistant, it is a legal requirement to have certain insurance and liability protection. Others are not compulsory, but are recommended because of the financial protection they provide. Photographers should be aware of the distinctions, so they are able to anticipate the point in their career when it is necessary to get cover from these policies.

There are fundamental differences between voluntary and legally required insurance and liability policies:

i) liability provides protection against claims made by other people (or companies) against a photographer, and will cover any payment awarded against the insured, in or out of court.

ii) insurance policies can protect virtually anything including individuals, income, premises, equipment, film, portfolio, car, home or personal possessions, from accident, damage, loss or theft, and claims are not usually dependent on a court decision.

This unit will provide details on different voluntary and compulsory general insurance covers and those policies specific to professional photography practice.

ELEMENT 1 : OPTIONAL INSURANCE POLICIES

Personal Accident Insurance (PAI)

Employees who have a contract of employment and pay Class 1 NI contributions are given protection at work from the National Insurance (Industrial Injuries) Act. In the case of an accident or injury which prevents them from being able to do their job, they are eligible to claim benefit until they are able to resume work. However, self-employed people do not receive the same protection unless they make their own provision and arrange cover with Personal Accident Insurance (PAI).

PAI differs from liability indemnity because it does not depend on the discretion of a court and proof that negligence caused the injury or accident. Most PAI policies will also provide cover for:

- 24 hours a day
- Worldwide (unlike liability cover)
- Death and Capital Benefits
- Temporary or total disablement.

But the small-print should always be carefully checked. These terms mean that even if a photographer is on vacation or working in the UK or abroad, at any time of the day or night, and suffers an accident which results in them being unable to work, they will receive payments until they are able to work again. The following points should be borne in mind:

i) PAI does not always cover sickness.

ii) PAI does not cover existing on-going injuries (eg. photographers frequently suffer back-problems) and the policy should start before any such complaints occur.

iii) Most PAI policies have a 7-day policy excess, although some may be longer. This means that they must be unable to work for more than a week (or longer) before a claim can be made.

iv) PAI will only provide compensation if loss of earnings can be proven (ie. an official art order confirming a job or, for assistants, a statement from a photographer saying that they had been booked as a freelance assistant for a job which injury prevents them from being able to do). Alternatively, the previous year's earnings may be taken into consideration.

v) If someone is involved in a 'hazardous activity' and an accident occurs, this may invalidate the PAI claim. Some policies will cover leisure skiing, but competition or racing events are excluded. As a general rule, any dangerous sport should be checked with the insurance company in order to consider whether extra cover is necessary.

Income Protection Insurance

Personal Accident Insurance can provide an income should an injury prevent a photographer from working, but it does not cover loss of income because of illness (see also u11:e9:p93). Banks and insurance companies offer various Income Protection Policies for both employees and the self-employed which can provide protection in case of illness.

These optional schemes can provide an income should earnings cease or be drastically reduced through long-term illness or physical disability, and supplement the basic Statutory Sick Pay employees may receive, and Sickness Benefit that the self-employed may receive. These state benefits are only available for a maximum of 28 weeks, but Income Protection Plan payments do not have such a limit.

For the self-employed, the monthly payments for Income Protection are assessed on net relevant earnings - that is income after deducting allowable business expenses (u7:e3:p64). Payments will be assessed on current income and the period chosen to defer payments once any income has ceased, and will provide up to 75% of earnings.

Loss of Business/Business Interruption

All businesses, including professional photographers, can insure their earning capacity. A photographer's earnings could become interrupted for various reasons, including the destruction of, or damage to, the equipment or the studio, or the photographer being injured or catching a disease. Material damage, resulting in the reduction in a photographer's turnover, is usually called 'business interruption', and the insurance cover will make up for any loss of turnover directly resulting from the loss of use of the damaged property.

In addition to the loss of turnover, and indeed to prevent such a loss, the photographer is also covered for costs incurred when hiring replacement equipment or a studio, as well as the cost of advising clients of any alterations. These items are known as 'additional cost of working' expenses. A policy covering loss of fees or gross profit will include both the above elements, ie. loss of turnover and additional costs of working. However, it is possible to select only the extra costs of working if the photographer feels that they will not suffer a loss of turnover.

The personal injury or sickness of the photographer (as opposed to material damage) can be covered by accident and sickness policies, which supply an income calculated to be the equivalent of net earnings.

Critical Illness

Critical Illness insurance is a fairly recent product which is now generally available. It was introduced to meet the needs of an individual should they contract a serious illness, and pays a lump sum, rather than a regular income. Payment is made on diagnosis, not on death, and the sum selected should take in to account any extra costs involved, eg. wheel chairs, home help, etc. It is important to check the scope of the policy, ie. the definition of the illness on which the policy will pay.

Motor Insurance Additional Premiums

Motor insurance is of course mandatory, however, there are certain additional voluntary premiums that should be considered if the vehicle is used as part of the business.

When photographers require an assistant (or any other person) to drive any business vehicle, it is the photographer's responsibility to provide adequate insurance cover for the occasion. Alternatively, an assistant may obtain cover so that they are insured to drive any vehicle for business or pleasure, so that they are certain of being covered. This can be expensive, so an assistant should always check the insurance status with a photographer before they drive their vehicle. Don't take risks with motor insurance and don't make assumptions about cover.

Weather Contingency

With escalating production costs, Weather Contingency Insurance is becoming increasingly popular with some photographers' clients. This cover indemnifies the photographer and his/her client against interruptions to and abandonment of shoots in exterior locations. Cover is usually for unreasonable photographic conditions, which can include rainfall, high winds and poor light. It is possible, at certain times of the year and in certain overseas places, to insure against lack of sunshine if sunlight is essential for a particular production. However, the costs are high but may be reduced by including a specified period of time before a claim can be made, for example two hours of rain before the interruption becomes claimable. It is normal practice to include weather insurance as a specific item in the budget, thereby passing the cost on to the client. Be aware that seven calendar days are required for an order on Weather Contingency Insurance.

Equipment Insurance

Most insurance brokers can provide insurance for loss, theft or damage to a photographer's equipment, but a firm which specialises in the film, TV and photography business is usually recommended. A complete list of all the insurable items should be submitted to the insurance agent with accurate information or current replacement values. These figures should be updated annually so that equipment is adequately covered. Policies can be arranged to protect equipment for:

- Studio only
- UK only
- UK and Europe
- Worldwide

Photographers are able to expand the cover if they are shooting outside the area normally covered, and pay an additional premium. If a photographer has to do this more than twice in a year, it is usually cheaper to upgrade the policy at the renewal date to include the additional area(s) on a permanent basis.

Some equipment policies automatically cover theft from the photographer's car, but individual policies may specify that cover is only during daylight hours or that the car should be fitted with a 'suitable' car alarm. However, some policies will exclude theft from a car altogether, and so policies should be considered very carefully to ensure that all the provision is suitable. Details should always be checked and nothing should be assumed.

Film Insurance

All risks policies will cover damage, loss or theft on raw stock, master negatives, prints, transparencies and like property whilst shooting in any specified territory (eg. UK or Europe etc).

It still continues to be the custom of the trade that contract conditions of processing laboratories, couriers, etc, exclude any claim for loss or damage, even if they are very clearly the culpable party. The onus is therefore on the photographer to take out insurance against events such as: the film becoming damaged during processing; the lab's courier losing the film whilst delivering it to the studio; or the film becoming damaged during printing.

Some laboratories carry insurance which protects the photographer, but this should always be seen in writing and compared with the overall trading terms and conditions.

Portfolio Insurance

The time and money invested in putting together a student portfolio is multiplied many times during the development and maintenance of a professional photographer's portfolio or 'book'. A portfolio will often be out of the photographer's or agent's care, custody or control and the personal and commercial value that it holds should be insured for. Most photographers pay an additional premium on their equipment insurance to cover their portfolios against loss, damage or theft. If you consider the times that a book will be with a courier or will be carried in the street or on public transport, insurance is essential. However, be aware that portfolio insurance only covers the cost of remounting a new portfolio and not the cost of reshooting the lost or damaged transparencies.

Photographers may worry about the time that their portfolio can spend in agency and design group reception areas. However, these companies have a duty of care (u3:e1:p33) and usually have specialised Commercial Combined Insurance policies which give all risks protection to many things, including film (neg and transparency), 'for which the insured has assumed responsibilities'.

Goods In Trust

Goods In Trust is a voluntary insurance policy which protects photographers against damage to props they have hired or borrowed. In the same way that Employer's Liability covers any person working under a photographer's 'care, custody & control', Goods In Trust provides the same protection for props and items temporarily under the photographer's care, custody and control.

These 'temporary' products and props cannot be covered on the studio contents insurance, nor on Public Liability policies. Many companies and freelance people in the industry should have Goods In Trust (u4:e8:p46) cover, whether they are stylists, home economists, design groups, advertising agencies, or any person/organisation that may be temporarily entrusted with someone else's property. In the case of a photographer, this is loosely referred to as 'props, sets and wardrobe'. Goods In Trust does not cover camera and lighting hire equipment; these are usually insured when the hire fee is paid, according to the hire agreement. The only exception to this is the insurance of hire studios, which are covered by the photographer's Public Liability and not Goods In Trust.

Goods In Trust is usually an addition to the photographer's studio contents insurance and is arranged to a limit agreed between the photographer and broker. Usual cover is for a specific amount between £1,000-£5,000 and the photographer is able to organise additional cover for items that go over this limit, such as a car or an expensive prop specially made by a model-maker.

It is a common mistake for a photographer to think that Public Liability cover (see opposite) will always protect them against damage to another person's property, caused by their negligence, during the course of a job. However, special circumstances of props and locations must always be considered and accounted for, before the day of the shoot.

Example 1a A photographer is on location in a stately home and is photographing an interior shot. They walk backwards, knock a valuable vase from a pedestal and smash it.

Possible Outcome The vase was not in the shot and would probably be covered under Public Liability Insurance.

Example 1b A photographer is on location in a stately home and is shooting an interior which features many valuable porcelain vases in situ. They knock one from the pedestal and it smashes.

Possible Outcome The vase was intrinsic to the shot and was therefore a prop. The photographer would not be covered under Public Liability but would have to make a claim on Goods In Trust. Negligence does not have to be proven in court before the insurance company will pay.

It is a common mistake to assume that Public Liability will provide cover for this situation because damage was done to another's property. However, anything that is featured in or is intrinsic to the photograph is considered to be a prop and therefore any damage would have to be claimed for under the photographer's Goods In Trust policy.

Example 2 A photographer hires a mirror from a specialist hire shop and arranges the invoicing and a courier to collect it. The mirror is collected by the courier company and taken to the photographer's studio. While the courier is closing the van doors, a member of the public walks into the mirror and damages part of the frame.

Possible Outcome This is more difficult to resolve and it would be up to the insurance companies to decide who was ultimately responsible for the damage. However, if the photographer or the courier had Goods In Trust insurance, no liability would have to be proven and no decision would have to be made by the court, and each insurance company will try to get the other(s) to pay the claim. The Goods In Trust policy should cover the replacement value of the mirror and frame.

Policy Excesses

All policies will vary but it is important to check the excess that is payable. An 'excess' is the amount the insured must contribute to a claim before any payment is made by the insurance company and applies to most insurance policies.

Example 1 A student/young photographer without a studio has £700 worth of equipment and gets a commercial equipment quote with an excess of £500 for a cost of £150. All the equipment is stolen and a claim is made and the insurance company pays the difference between the excess and the claim. The insured receives a cheque for £200 but has already paid a £150 premium and must still pay the £500 in order to replace the equipment.

In this case, the policy was obviously not suitable and a household contents policy with a smaller excess would probably have been sufficient, pending clearance from the underwriters. The camera equipment could have been listed as named items on the general household contents policy. However, should this limited amount of equipment be used for any commercial purpose, it is necessary to declare it to the insurance company, no matter what its value is.

Example 2 A photographer with £15,000 worth of equipment has commercial equipment insurance with a £100 excess for an average premium of £350 (UK only). It would not be permissible to include this equipment on a household contents policy.

This policy is more suitable to the photographer's needs and is therefore more viable.

ELEMENT 2 : PUBLIC LIABILITY INSURANCE

Public Liability Insurance is not compulsory. However, policies will protect a photographer from a situation where the photographer's proven negligence causes:

- loss or damage to property;
- disease, death or injury to another person (third party injury).

Example A photographer is shooting on location in a busy street and a member of the public trips over a lighting cable and injures themselves and decides to seek compensation from the photographer.

A court would have to decide whether the accident was caused because of the photographer's negligence (was the shooting area sufficiently cordoned off? were the cables secured properly to the ground? etc.) and whether the claim against the photographer is justified.

If the photographer does not have public liability cover, they will have to meet the costs of defending an action and the additional costs of lawyer's fees. Public Liability means that all costs are handled by the insurance company, no matter what the outcome of the claim.

Public Liability will usually only cover an incident which would be heard in a UK court; if shooting abroad, refer to Element 5, page 81.

ELEMENT 3 : EMPLOYER'S LIABILITY INSURANCE

All employers must, by law, have Employer's Liability Insurance. The definition of an 'employee' in this case is often unclear and this may cause confusion, but it is generally understood to be any one working under someone's 'care, custody and control', whether or not a fee is being paid for the person's services (u7:e1:p61). This can include:

- a person under contract of service or apprenticeship;
- a person employed by labour only sub-contractors;
- a self-employed person;
- a person hired to, or borrowed by, the insured;
- a person undertaking study or work experience.

Employer's Liability protects the photographer from any claim of death, bodily injury or disease to an employee arising during a job. If action is taken by an 'employee' who has suffered, say, injury, and the court decides that the photographer was negligent and therefore liable, Employer's Liability will meet the costs of the action and also the compensation. However, if they don't have a valid policy they will be liable for all costs, fees and compensation and face prosecution for not having Employer's Liability.

Like Public Liability, Employer's Liability provides cover in the UK Nationals only (see Element 5 if shooting abroad).

Photographic Assistants and Public & Employer's Liability

The reasons are clear why a professional photographer should have Public & Employer's Liability, but consider the implications for a photographic assistant. The fact that no fee need be paid to an 'employee' means that, whenever an assistant tests to update their portfolio, there may be other people involved acting under their 'care, custody and control', such as models, stylists, set-builders or even a friend who is assisting. Should any of them suffer injury and the photographer/assistant is negligent, they may be liable. Any assistant involved in such activities should also have Employers' Liability protection.

Similarly, if a photographer's/assistant's proven negligence damages someone's property whilst testing or shooting for themselves, Public Liability insurance will provide for any payments awarded against them and legal costs incurred.

ELEMENT 4 : PROFESSIONAL INDEMNITY INSURANCE

Professional Indemnity Insurance is considered essential protection for all professional practices in today's litigious climate. Photographers are at risk in the same way as other professional practitioners to claims arising from professional negligence. Incidents of an apparently minor nature could ultimately result in substantial court awards and expensive legal costs. Cover enables you to reduce the financial effect of such claims on your business, and protect your livelihood.

Professional Indemnity Cover

The cover can be comprehensive and include your liability at law for the following essential features:

- any neglect, error or omission by you, your employees or agents;
- infringement of property or contract rights;
- libel, slander, defamation or violation of copyright law;
- dishonesty of employees or agents.

And in addition:

- fees and expenses which a client would have paid to you, but for your mistake;
- additional costs incurred by you to rectify a mistake;
- the costs of replacing lost or destroyed films, photographs and documents;
- compensation for court attendance at £100 per day;
- legal defence costs.

Indemnity is usually limited to £250,000 for any one claim. Claims can arise from a wide variety of areas, but here are just a few situations which could produce a claim against you:

- the film, camera or processing is defective so no photographs are available for the client, resulting in a reshoot;
- the photographs become lost in the post or in transit;
- an engagement is omitted from your diary or you turn up at the wrong place or at the wrong time;
- libel or slander.

It is impossible to estimate how much these claims could cost, but any commercial dispute is likely to cost in excess of £300, and substantially more will be involved if solicitors are engaged or if you have to reshoot a large job.

Exclusions

There are very few exclusions with Professional Indemnity Cover, however, you cannot cover a claim arising from circumstances of which you were aware when you took out the policy, and you will be asked to make a specific contribution to each claim. Cover can only be granted to independent photographers (including partnerships and limited companies) and not to employees. Employees should be protected by their employer's policy.

ELEMENT 5 : WORKING ABROAD

Employer's Liability

Employer's Liability Insurance cover is normally on a worldwide basis for employees who are UK citizens; however, if you go abroad to shoot and employ local residents, you will have to take out local insurance in that particular country, in advance, particularly the USA. For example, if a photographer is shooting in Miami and has taken UK models to the USA for the job, the photographer will be covered in the event of any accident to the models caused by the photographer's negligence by Employer's Liability. However, if local models were used instead, it would be necessary to have additional US cover.

Public Liability

Special provisions need to be made, prior to the job, for work done abroad (especially in the USA). Public Liability Insurance cover is normally worldwide, excluding the USA and Canada, but most insurers will extend cover for these areas if requested. If local cover is preferred, the names of insurance companies that deal with commercial liability can be obtained from embassies and consulates in this country.

Often when photographers work in the USA, they are requested to note the interest of, or co-insure, third parties on their policy, which can be problematical. Insurers will note third party interests, but may request additional premiums for doing so. British Insurers will not co-insure a third party, so if this cannot be avoided, you will have to organise American Insurance, which can prove expensive.

Never presume you have sufficient insurance cover - always check before you travel.

SUMMARY

Photographers usually deal with one insurance agent or broker and have all their required policies on one annual schedule, to make administration more simple.

Insurance and Liability are an essential part of a business and it is important not to avoid what is a legal requirement. To do so can incur much greater penalties in the long run.

It is also important to consider those optional and advised insurance policies outlined above. However, it is too easy to calculate just the costs of these and not what is at stake if cover isn't arranged. A lack of or inadequate cover can affect more than just the photographer's finances, but also the lives and income of people working with them.

Unit 10 : Collecting Societies

INTRODUCTION

Until recently, photographers have managed their rights for themselves or through an agent or specialist photographic library. With increases in mass use of photographs, photographers have looked towards a solution which composers, musicians and authors have for many years known about: the collecting society.

This unit provides the photographer with background information on collecting societies and their purpose, and demonstrates how such societies can help photographers to manage and control their rights. Collecting societies are increasingly important in the digital world and photographers should understand their role and purpose before they need the support which collecting societies offer to the creator community.

ELEMENT 1 : BRIEF BACKGROUND TO COLLECTING SOCIETIES

Collecting societies are not a new phenomenon; they have long existed for the creators of music, who in the early years of this century were concerned that, with the advent of broadcasting and recording, mass use of their works would overwhelm their rights. They created collecting societies to work for them. In more recent years, with developments in photocopying, authors and publishers joined together to develop an agency, the Copyright Licensing Agency (CLA), which could licence photocopying of books and journals, particularly for educational use.

Collecting societies for visual artists are also well established in other European countries. In some cases this has resulted from the need for collective administration of rights, such as droit de suite (the artists' resale right), which does not currently exist in the UK. In other countries, where licensing schemes are governed by legislation, collecting societies were needed which represented all types of creators, and artists and photographers were included from the beginning.

The Design and Artists Copyright Society (DACS) has existed in the UK since 1983, but for most of that time it has managed the copyright of fine artists on an individual basis. Such artists do not make the main part of their livelihood from reproduction rights but from the sale of their works, and so turn to the visual arts' collecting societies for the administration of their reproduction rights.

Until recently, a collecting society for the visual arts as a whole seemed largely irrelevant, and their activities were peripheral to those of the illustrator, designer or photographer working commercially. Of much more importance for those creators were their agents and photographic libraries, but again, pressure for mass use of works is forcing a change, and for the administration of certain rights photographers are turning to the collecting society and the solutions it offers.

This pressure has come from the need to find new solutions for the management and administration of rights in the digital environment, and in looking for these solutions visual creators have realised they are entitled to a share from other rights already collectively administered, such as photocopying or secondary broadcasting.

It should be strongly emphasised, that the collecting society does not replace traditional forms of representation for the artist, rather it complements the work of the agent and photographic library and provides additional strands of income for the photographer.

ELEMENT 2 : WHAT IS A COLLECTING SOCIETY?

Collecting societies normally, although not always, operate as non-profit making companies, and most are membership organisations with members from the repertoire they represent, for example, DACS' repertoire is creators of artistic works (including photographers). Collecting societies are governed by a board of management made up of elected members of the society working to rules established in their Memorandum and Articles of Association. The board of management works closely with a specialist employed administration.

The aims of most collecting societies are to work for the benefit of their members and of the repertoire they represent; enshrined within their Memorandum and Articles of Association are educational and charitable objectives. Most importantly, they have a mandate from their members to represent their copyright.

The membership agreement between the collecting society and each individual member, grants to the Society the exclusive right to represent some, or all, of that member's copyright interests.

For fine artists, DACS represents all areas of copyright, including the main reproduction rights. For a photographer, DACS is more likely to represent what are known as 'secondary rights'.

The collecting society acts on behalf of the artist or photographer, negotiating fees and granting licences for the reproduction or broadcast of works, either on a case by case basis or through a licensing scheme. The collecting society deducts a commission from the fee and pays a royalty to the member. Collecting societies have other functions: education has already been mentioned, and they carry out lobbying activities at national, European and international levels. They also police the marketplace on behalf of members, and infringements of copyright are vigorously pursued.

Collecting societies operate internationally through a network of similar societies, bound together by reciprocal agreements which allow each society to represent the members of the other societies within its territory of representation. For example, VG Bild-Kunst in Germany has a reciprocal agreement with DACS in the UK through which each represents the other's members. The network of visual arts collecting societies represents over 40,000 artists worldwide and includes some of the most prestigious names in 20th Century art.

ELEMENT 3 : SECONDARY RIGHTS

'Secondary rights' are those rights which collecting societies are best placed to administer for artists and photographers working in commercial art. They are those rights which are exercised subsequent to the first or primary use of a photograph. For example, a photograph which has been licensed for reproduction in a book (primary use) may subsequently be photocopied (secondary use). Secondary rights are rights which are difficult or, in some cases, impossible for the photographer or artist to control as an individual. These rights are normally managed for the photographer by a collecting society. The collecting society, as the mandated representative of a large group of copyright owners, negotiates collectively with a user, such as a major broadcaster, or a user group, such as an association representing educational establishments. A licence agreement is issued by the collecting society for the use of the entire repertoire. The user pays a lump sum, often based on factors other than actual use of works, and also provides usage data, perhaps in the form of statistical data or surveys which help to identify relevant copyright owners.

The collecting society is then responsible for ensuring that the user complies with the terms of the agreement, and for allocating and distributing revenue to the repertoire.

The list of secondary rights which DACS includes in its membership agreement are as follows:

- cable retransmission right
- those digital and electronic imaging rights administered collectively
- lending right
- off-air recording right
- private audio-visual right
- public display right
- rental right
- reprographic right
- resale right (droit de suite)
- satellite broadcast right

Some of these rights do not yet apply in the UK, although they do in other parts of Europe. Others exist, but negotiations for a share for the visual arts have only recently commenced, whilst DACS is already receiving revenue for others.

ELEMENT 4 : HOW COLLECTING SOCIETIES LICENCE

The 1988 Copyright Act provides for collecting societies under the sections relating to licensing bodies and licensing schemes, and their activities are regulated by the Copyright Tribunal. However, there is little legislation which directly controls how they operate their schemes or what licences they are able to offer. This is not the case in other parts of Europe, particularly in Scandinavia.

Often, licensing schemes not only include the members of the collecting society, but also provide a form of insurance for the user against claims by non-members who are part of the repertoire; this is known as indemnification. Membership of collecting societies is normally voluntary and it is virtually impossible for any collecting society to represent 100% of the repertoire through its membership agreements. However, users need to be sure that they are fully protected against claims for copyright infringement. By offering indemnification to the user, the collecting society takes responsibility for satisfying claims in relation to use by non members, as long as that use was within the terms of the licence provided to the user.

ELEMENT 5 : DESIGN AND ARTISTS COPYRIGHT SOCIETY (DACS)

DACS has already been referred to as the collecting society for visual artists in the UK and since 1992, it has been actively working towards the establishment of a strong membership for secondary rights. During that time it has received mandates from a large number of professional organisations representing a wide variety of artists, from photographers to cartoonists and strip illustrators, from photojournalists to sculptors, and it now represents some 8,000 artists and photographers in matters of secondary rights in the UK.

Secondary membership of DACS is open to any creator of artistic works. There is no joining or membership fee for secondary members, but DACS does deduct a commission for its administrative costs from any revenue distributed for secondary rights.

DACS has not yet made a distribution of secondary revenue, but it is developing the computer and administration systems which will enable it to distribute revenue accumulated from secondary rights by the end of 1997. Recognising that it is accountable to the whole of the visual arts repertoire and not just to its members, DACS has established a Distribution Policy Working Group made up of representatives of the supporting professional organisations. This Group is developing a distribution policy which will ensure that distribution of secondary revenue will be equitable.

Many collecting societies are large organisations controlling many millions of pounds of revenue. As yet, DACS is small but is growing rapidly. Photographers should join DACS - their collecting society - to ensure that, through this membership organisation, they have a say in what rights are managed, how they are managed, and how this revenue is allocated and distributed to the photographic sector.

Unit 11 : Advanced Business

INTRODUCTION

Whether you plan to work alone or employ other people, running a business requires a ground knowledge of all the options open to you to be a success. This unit aims to initiate the photographer into the world of 'how to succeed in business - and stay there'. It explores the various savings and investment schemes, pensions, financial advice and mortgages, and advises on claiming benefit during the hard times.

ELEMENT 1 : SOLE TRADER; PARTNERSHIP; LIMITED COMPANY

Sole Trader

Most photographers work as sole traders. This is probably the simplest way to trade. It gives you the greatest freedom over your actions, and does not preclude you from taking on employees if you want or need to.

There are disadvantages to being a sole trader. You are personally liable for all your business debts, and your risk of bankruptcy if your business fails is greater than for traders working through a Limited Company (see below). Another disadvantage to being a sole trader is that you have no-one else to share your responsibilities with.

All businesses need to understand that an invoice, say for £1,000, is not the photographer's personal money. It belongs to the business, and business costs need to be met from it before the profit element can be spent (or saved). Failure to maintain this simple discipline can end up in disaster.

Partnership

Partnerships also have unlimited liability for debts, and each partner can bind the other. The partners are jointly and severally liable for the debts of the business. Business partnerships should not be entered into lightly. It is crucial for there to be a proper written agreement between the partners, drawn up with the help of a solicitor. However well the individual partners get on with each other at the beginning, unforseen problems can and do occur (death, illness, copyright ownership, pursuit of other interests, etc.). Preparation is better and cheaper than litigation.

Limited Company

Limited companies are formal companies registered under one of the Companies Acts and are separate legal entities in their own right. Company assets belong to the company and not to the shareholders, so if a company fails and goes into liquidation, the shareholders and directors would not normally be entitled to any of the company's assets (equipment, copyrights, etc.). These would be sold for the benefit of the people owed money by the company. The main advantages and disadvantages of a company are:

a) Liability for debts cannot normally be claimed against directors and shareholders unless personal guarantees are given. Personal guarantees are almost invariably required nowadays by banks and other lending companies.
b) The company is perpetual, until it is wound up. It is not affected by directors coming or going, unlike partnerships which may be dissolved by, for example, the death of a partner. The company's shareholders (owners) can sell their shares.
c) The bureaucracy surrounding a company is substantial. Small companies no longer require an annual audit, but accounts have to be filed at Companies House according to a strict deadline, or fines will result; and forms need to be completed when there is a change of directors, company secretary or shareholders.
d) A company can have its freedom to act restricted by its rules (Memorandum and Articles of Association).

If you decide to form a Limited Company, you must make sure that copyright in your images is vested with you and not your company. As a Limited Company there are two ways in which you can opt to be paid and this is important in assessing the ownership of copyright:

- as an employee, paying yourself a wage/salary with tax and national insurance paid through PAYE;
- by dividend, payable weekly or monthly.

Both payment methods have their own advantages and disadvantages which would be specific to your business, and advice should be sought as to which one is right for you.

On the copyright issue, should you decide to pay yourself a dividend, you are not an 'employed person' and you therefore own the copyright in your images. On the other hand, should you decide to pay yourself as an employee, under the Copyright Designs and Patents Act 1988 the owner of the copyright is your employer - your company. Should the company go into receivership or liquidation, the copyright in your images becomes an asset of the company.

The way to resolve this problem is to have a document drawn up, before you begin trading, to establish the ownership of copyright. This may be in the form of an assignment by the company to you; but to ensure there are no loopholes we would recommend getting the document drawn up by a lawyer. If you are already a Limited Company and have not made arrangements for copyright ownership, legal advice should be sought as to the best way to now formally assign the copyright to you. You may find that you have to buy the copyright as it has a value as a company asset, but it is worth looking into to prevent future wrangles.

ELEMENT 2 : BOOKKEEPING

Bookkeeping has been mentioned in Units 7 and 8 on VAT and Tax. Whether computerised or handwritten, well managed and up to date books of account can quickly provide you with information about how well your business is doing, as well as satisfying the tax authorities!

Many photographers contract their main bookkeeping to specialised bookkeepers, either directly, or via their accountants. This has the advantage of removing the worry of having to do the work themselves when other business is more pressing (as well as ensuring that VAT Returns are ready on time). The main disadvantage, particularly to the photographer just starting out, is cost. However, if you get (and heed) advice from your accountant, you should be able to maintain your own accounts books in a straightforward way.

Accountants keep records in several different ways. One example of a cash book, which is a record of your expenditure and income through your bank account, is shown as illustrations 16 and 17 on pages 139 and 141. You will also need a petty cash book; this should be used for recording cash and credit card expenditure (*ill 18:p143*).

Sales need to be recorded properly and again an example is given (*ill 19:p145*). Good sales and payments records will show who owes you money, enabling you to keep an eye on slow payers. Records of your purchases paid by cheque also need to be kept meticulously, with suppliers bills both paid and unpaid filed properly.

Don't throw anything away! All books and records must be kept for up to eight years, depending on when your accounts period starts. The authorities can impose large fines if records are lost or destroyed.

Good advice from your accountant before you start can save you money on accountancy fees later on, as well as giving you peace of mind, knowing that bookkeeping is one less thing to worry about.

ELEMENT 3 : CREDIT CONTROL

Poor credit control can result in failure of a business and possibly bankruptcy. Your clients often cynically look on you as a cheap form of finance. Most photographers don't charge interest, unlike their bankers, so by not paying up for a long time, they save themselves a lot of money.

Credit control is something you need to tackle early on in the life of your business and the policy you adopt needs to be stuck to. Your credit terms need to be stated clearly on the bottom of each invoice (eg. Terms Net, 30 days. Interest will be charged at 4% over 'xyz' bank's base rate on all accounts which are more than 30 days overdue).

Your sales records need to be checked monthly against payments received and statements should be sent on a regular basis to clients who have not paid their outstanding accounts. These statements should be backed up with telephone calls to the accounts departments of the companies concerned. Photographers dealing with advertising agencies and publishing groups should not fear treading on the toes of their clients as the creative departments usually have little to do with the accounts departments of these organisations. You need to find a contact name in the relevant accounts department and if necessary harass that person until your overdue account is settled. Daily telephone calls can work wonders. If you shout louder than the next person you are more likely to get paid, if only so that they get rid of the nuisance (you!). If you have used the correct paperwork, including terms and conditions (*ill 2:p108*), the use of your image is dependent on your being paid; the client could be in breach of copyright.

If an account becomes seriously overdue, you should consider the threat of legal action. Debts of up to £3,000 can be taken to the small claims court, and up to £50,000 to a County Court. Small claims courts are a cheap way of bringing matters to a head, as they only involve minimal legal costs. All County Courts issue leaflets on what to do and what forms you will have to complete to start a small claim. Your local County Court will be listed in the telephone directory under 'Courts'.

You can threaten an individual who owes you more than £750 with the prospect of bankruptcy and, via a solicitor, commence bankruptcy proceedings. You can also threaten a limited company with the prospect of having it wound up. A formal letter such as this, particularly from a solicitor, ought to have a pretty salutory effect.

You may be trading very successfully, but if people are not paying you for the work that you do you cannot pay your suppliers or your own living expenses. You would not expect your suppliers to tolerate your not paying them.

ELEMENT 4 : OPENING ACCOUNTS WITH SUPPLIERS

Paying cash on delivery for all business purchases is not advisable business practice, and you will therefore need to open accounts with major suppliers.

To open an account you will first need to obtain an application form. This will ask for your name, address, length of time trading, etc., as well as for two trade references, your bank details and the amount of credit required (your supplier will double this amount when seeking trade references as you will always owe him for both the current and previous month's purchases). The trade references you give should be companies you already have credit accounts with. If this is your first account, give a personal reference, but make sure both your name and your business name are quoted on the form.

Many suppliers include, as part of their application form, a declaration or reference to their Terms & Conditions of Sale; by signing the application, you agree to abide by these terms. The terms cover the supplier's obligations, liabilities, payment terms, penalties and other areas, which ensure suppliers are legally protected against pretty well everything. These do not normally present a problem but should always be checked before signing.

ELEMENT 5 : BORROWING MONEY

Most businesses have to borrow money at one time or another, for example, to finance a new piece of equipment or a large job where payment is likely to be received after costs have been incurred. Often a short term bank overdraft can be arranged without fuss, but always ask first. If you continually overdraw without permission you are unlikely to be welcomed with open arms when you want more substantial finance. You also run the risk of being asked to close your account and will be charged a penal rate of interest.

Companies supplying equipment, motor vehicles and so on, are often keen to offer finance because they get commission from the finance company who provide the money for the transaction. Interest rates on such transactions are often, but not always, higher than the rates charged by banks.

Banks are the natural source of finance, both short and long term, and are often the best place to go. Cash in your pocket enables you to negotiate better terms with the equipment supplier, reducing the overall cost of the transaction. The down side is that banks often demand a great deal from borrowers - particularly new businesses - and they still have a long way to go before they shake off the commonly held opinion that they are heavy handed. Except for small sums, banks often want security, such as personal guarantees for loans. They also want to see accounts to back up claims of business viability. Cash flow statements and detailed business plans are also required by many bank managers before they will consider a loan.

Businesss Plans

A business plan is a projection of how you think your business will develop in the future. It is normally split into trading years (twelve month periods) and covers any period from one to five years depending on its purpose. In the context of sole traders, it should also include a summary of personal expenditure so that the business profits and cash flow can be related to domestic circumstances.

The object of a business plan is to calculate in advance what your financial requirements might be during the next twelve months and to enable you to plan your cash flow and expenditure sensibly, thus being prepared for problems before they arise.

When preparing a business plan, the best advice is to stick to the rule 'what in your heart of hearts do you really think will happen'. If you are over-optimistic on fees, or reduce your expenses unrealistically to show an improved profit for any reason, you will only lead yourself into cash flow problems; your Bank Manager will lose confidence in you and you may end up spending money which you do not have.

Most major banks publish booklets spelling out what they want from your business plan. These booklets are very detailed and sophisticated in their scope and offer much advice and help, as well as showing you how to present the information they require before deciding to lend you money.

ELEMENT 6 : FACTORING

Factoring is a way of turning your sales into cash before your clients pay you. In practice you borrow the bulk of each invoice you issue. Factoring companies are often subsidaries of major banks. Factoring (or invoice discounting) companies buy your unpaid invoices as they arise and pay you up to 80% of their value, with the balance, less adminstrative and finance charges, being paid to you when your clients pay their invoices. They also advise on credit risks and potential bad debts. However, factoring is expensive and should only be considered as a last resort, and a factoring arrangement should not be entered into without first discussing it with your accountant.

Factoring companies will not normally deal with new businesses. They want to see a turnover in excess of £50,000 and an established trading record. Their service is designed to improve cash flow, but they can be expensive.

See Useful Address (page 148) for The Association of British Factors and Associates.

ELEMENT 7 : PRIZES AND AWARDS

Prizes and awards related to your profession, and particularly awards you have entered for, are normally taxable income, for example, a golfer or snooker player would pay tax on prize money as well as appearance money. Any such prize should be entered on your Tax Return. However, a prize given to you by a third party, and for which you did not enter, would not normally be taxed (eg. Booker Prize).

ELEMENT 8 : LEASING AND ASSET FINANCE

The pros and cons of where to borrow money from are dealt with in Element 5 of this unit. Borrowing money so as to pay cash for a piece of equipment may result in obtaining a good discount, thereby reducing the financial cost of the deal.

Leasing or hire purchase may be a suitable alternative, and homework needs to be done before a decision can be made. The main points to be taken into consideration are:

a) The cheapest cost of borrowing money to pay for equipment.
b) Your ability and desire to provide security.
c) Cash flow and tax considerations.

Hire Purchase
Hire purchase is an agreement whereby goods are hired to you over a period. You then obtain ownership of the goods for a nominal sum. You can claim capital allowances (depreciation) for tax purposes, based on the cost of the goods.

Lease Purchase
A lease purchase is a commercial form of hire purchase and not a form of leasing. In both cases, hire and lease, the interest costs are a tax allowable business expense.

Contract Hire or Leasing
Contract hire or leasing is usually for a fixed period and the hire cost is high reflecting the capital cost of the asset. The hirer retains ownership throughout, and the hire costs are again a tax allowable business expense.

HP and leasing companies normally carry out rigorous checks into credit worthiness before entering into an agreement, but they do not normally require any security. You need to check the APR interest rate of the different types of deal before you sign any agreement. Your accountant should be able to help you if required.

Remember that, in the current economic climate, salesmen will exert a lot of pressure on you to take their 'deal'. Their commission is high, and business is slow. You have to live with what you agree, so don't be pressurised into signing something you are not sure of.

ELEMENT 9 : PENSIONS, SAVINGS, INVESTMENTS AND MORTGAGES

Pensions

With tax relief of up to 40% on contributions, no tax charges on the investment funds, and the facility to take a significant portion of the eventual benefits tax free, pensions are the most tax efficient investment format available in the UK. However, with the ever contracting state pension scheme, the importance of ensuring adequate personal provision for retirement is ever greater.

Since the introduction of personal pensions in 1987, there is much greater flexibility available in respect of how contributions can be made, what investments can be held, and when benefits can be taken. Anybody who is self-employed or not in an employer's pension scheme can take out a personal pension.

The maximum contribution allowable is calculated as a percentage of your net relevant earnings dependant on your age.

Age on 6th April	*% of net relevant earning*
35 or under	17.5
36 to 45	20.0
46 to 50	25.0
51 to 55	30.0
56 to 60	35.0
61 and over	40.0

It is possible to go back up to six years to utilise unused tax relief, which is particularly useful when making lump sum contributions.

All contributions within these limits qualify for tax relief at your highest marginal rate. The self-employed make pension contributions on a gross basis, which will then off-set part of the profits made in that year, thus directly reducing the eventual tax bill. Using pension contributions to off-set tax at the higher rate (40%) represents good value and self-employed individuals often make lump sum contributions after the end of their financial year equal to the profits taxed at 40%. There is provision to elect to have the Revenue treat the contribution as having been paid in the previous year to enable this technique to work.

Contributions can be made either on a monthly basis, or as a lump sum annually or individually. For those who have an erratic income profile, it is difficult to estimate what your likely profits will be and therefore what your pension contribution should be. Equally, the availability of a lump sum to make a contribution at the year end is not assured. The use of a combination of regular and single contributions is usually the best solution.

Personal Pensions can be used as a repayment vehicle for a mortgage in place of an endowment or capital and interest. This enables you to gain advantage from the tax efficiencies available. Up to 25% of the fund accrued at retirement can be taken as a tax free cash sum and it is this that is used to repay the mortgage. The other 75% of the fund is then used to pay an income in retirement. A pension fund has to be four times larger than the loan and yet, once tax relief is applied, contributions are generally only between 10% and 30% more than an equivalent endowment that only repays the loan. The high level of tax efficiency that pensions offer enables two tasks - loan repayment and retirement provision - to be employed at little extra cost compared to endowments or repayment mortgages.

Although pension contribution levels tend to be driven by tax mitigation, it is important to ensure that the eventual benefits are sufficient to meet your income needs in retirement. Estimates of benefits produced by particular contribution rates can be quite accurate if appropriate estimates of fund growth and inflation are used. This information will be a useful guide to the level of contribution needed to fulfil your requirements. You will also be able to plan for retirement at a particular age; however, whilst benefits can be taken from a personal pension from age 50 onwards, producing the necessary income at that age requires high contribution levels from a relatively young age.

For most people, their pension fund at retirement is their second largest asset behind their home. It is therefore essential that the investment strategy is correct. Investment funds covering the whole range of risk profiles are available, from low-risk 'with profits' funds to higher risk/potentially higher return funds, investing direct into world-wide stock markets. Whilst higher risk funds are an acceptable part of the portfolio when you have in excess of 10 years before retirement, there should always be a transition to low risk investments as retirement approaches.

For the more sophisticated investor with large pension assets, a self-invested personal pension provides a high level of personal investment control. Direct holdings of equities selected personally or with a stock broker, can be held, as can commercial property, even that used as your own business premises.

The inclusion of waiver-of-premium in a pension contract is crucial for the self employed, as this will maintain the contributions in the event that you are unable to work due to long term illness. As you would have no net relevant earnings during that time, pension contributions can not be continued in any other way.

For those trading as a limited company, the types of pension contract available and the maximum contribution calculations are very different. The use of an executive pension scheme or small self-administered scheme will enable contributions of up to 100% of salary to be made in certain circumstances. It is also possible to borrow from the scheme for business purposes.

When selecting which company you should use as your pension provider, it is essential that you assess the charges they levy and their performance prowess. The difference made to your eventual benefits by using a high-charging or under-performing company is enormous.

Savings & Investment

The creation and effective investment of a capital resource is of particular importance to those in business on their own account, be it for short term purposes, such as meeting an impending tax liability, creating a financial safety-net, or a specific medium term purpose such as school fees planning. There are several investment formats that offer tax free status to the investor. Use of these will boost the overall return on your capital.

National Savings Certificates
National Savings Certificates are available on either fixed interest or index-linked, 5 year rates. An investor can buy up to £10,000 of each issue. A reduced interest rate is applied on early exit.

Tax Exempt Special Savings Accounts
Tax Exempt Special Savings Accounts (TESSAs) enable you to hold building society deposits tax free. Up to £9,000 can be paid into a TESSA over its 5 year term, subject to a maximum

of £3,000 in the first year and £1,800 each year thereafter. Although the tax exemption is lost if your capital is withdrawn within 5 years, TESSAs almost always offer the highest deposit rates and should therefore be used where possible.

Personal Equity Plans
Personal Equity Plans (PEPs) were introduced in 1986 to encourage wider share ownership. They have evolved over recent years into a very low charging format offering a very wide investment choice, from non-risk, guaranteed corporate bond funds, to high risk Japanese Equity funds. Up to £6,000 can be placed into a General PEP each financial year, with a further £3,000 into a Single Company PEP. Regular savings schemes start from as little as £50.00 per month.

Having utilised your tax exempt savings allowances where appropriate, further investments can be made potentially tax free by using one of the investment formats whose growth is taxed as capital gains. Each individual can make gains of £6,300 (96/7 rate) each year without liability to tax. Investments of this type are:

Unit Trusts
Types of funds available are similar to those for PEPs, although no maximum holding applies. Sums of more than £10,000 are usually best held as part of a portfolio with several diverse holdings.

Investment Trusts
Broadly similar to Unit Trusts, although several different types of share are available, from geared Capital Shares or Income Shares to low risk Zero Dividend Preference Shares which are very useful for meeting known future liabilities.

Regular savings schemes for both Unit Trusts and Investment Trusts start from £50.00 per month. For investors with larger portfolios and higher incomes, there are several other areas offering tax mitigation for higher rate tax or roll-over relief for capital gains. These include:

Permanent Interest-Bearing Shares (PIBS)
A fixed-interest Building Society stock.

Enterprise Investment Schemes (EIS)
Partial income tax relief and capital gains tax relief on investments in unquoted companies.

Venture Capital Trusts (VCTs)
20% income tax and 40% capital gains re-investment relief and tax free dividends on the first £100,000.

The use of gross interest paying off-shore accounts in highly regulated territories such as the Isle of Man or Luxembourg, is becoming a widely used medium and offers significant advantages to investors with holdings of more than £30,000.

Having invested in several of the formats listed above, it is essential to ensure that the risk profile of your portfolio as a whole matches your expectations.

Income Replacement

The revision of the State Invalidity Benefit structure in April 1995, and in particular the end of mortgage benefit after 12 months, has highlighted the need to ensure that, should you be prevented from working due to illness or injury, you receive income at an appropriate level. Permanent Health insurance will provide an income in this event, up to a maximum of 75% of your Net Relevant Earnings. You can elect for a time delay between the beginning of the illness and the payments starting of 4, 8, 13, 26 and 52 weeks - the longer this deferment period, the cheaper the cost of cover. The interim period should be covered by capital reserves or work-in-progress. Payments continue until you are able to return to work or you reach your elected retirement age.

With effect from 6th April 1996, all benefit payments from individual permanent health insurance schemes are wholly exempt from tax.

Great care should be taken to ensure that any policy you effect will pay out in the event of your illness or injury preventing you from practising as a photographer, not on the basis of 'any' occupation.

Whilst Critical Illness contracts are no substitute for an Income Replacement contract they are very useful for creating capital to repay mortgages and loans and provide for a change in life-style in the event of diagnosis of a serious illness such as cancer, Multiple Sclerosis, etc. Where Income Replacement pays for non-life threatening illnesses and injuries, conversely, Critical Illness benefit can be received at a time when you are still able to work but perhaps would rather not (see also u9:e1d:p76).

Financial Advice

The Financial Services Act of 1986 created two distinct forms of financial adviser:

- The Tied Agent or Company Representative, who is limited to using the products of the Insurance Company or Bank for whom they work;
- Independent financial advisers, who are subject to regulations designed to ensure that they advise you on the best product available, across the whole financial market place, to meet your needs. Solicitors and accountants who offer financial advice can only do so on this basis.

It is not the case that all of one group is necessarily better than the other, as an effective financial adviser will be one that you personally like and trust and is appropriately qualified.

In theory, an independent adviser should be able to save you money by finding the cheapest rates for life insurance or income replacement, and by ensuring that only the most cost effective providers are used for pensions, PEPs, etc.

A good financial adviser should be able to offer you consistent advice over a number of years and in sympathy with your other advice, such as your accountant's and solicitor's. The most effective way to choose an adviser is either in conjunction with your accountant or a colleague who has experienced the advice given by the firm in question over a reasonable time period.

Many accountants and solicitors have ceased to provide direct advice due to the time commitment required to meet the qualifications necessary in addition to their own work.

All advisers are now obliged to inform you of the costs associated with the recommendation they make, and many independent financial advisers are happy to work on a fee basis similar to accountants.

The selection of an adviser capable of delivering high quality advice on pensions, investments, lending and insurances, without too much impact on your time, can be of enormous advantage if the right adviser for you is chosen.

Commercial Lending

The purchase of a commercial property, such as a studio, on a free-hold or long lease-hold basis, can not only make you money as an appreciating asset, but can also help your cash-flow if the loan is structured properly, relative to renting on equivalent premises.

Loans of up to 75% of property value are available on owner-occupied premises, however, in the circumstances where you are purchasing the free-hold of a property on which you hold a short lease, a higher percentage can be borrowed.

When approaching a potential lending source, it is essential that you show your finances are in harmony with the lender's requirements and that you have a clear idea of how you want the loan structured. Lenders are looking for ability to service the loan; so items such as current rent can be added back into your profits in most cases. The greater the ease with which the loan servicing can be met, the more competitive the interest rate you will be offered. Short and long term fixed rates, together with discounted and variable rates from 1% over base, are available.

The use of a pension scheme to purchase a commercial property offers several advantages. Firstly, you are able to utilise your current pension fund as a deposit (the balance being borrowed in the normal way) and, secondly, all rental income and any growth in property value are not subject to tax.

This facility has long been available to those trading as a limited company using a small self-administered scheme, but is now available to sole-traders/partners using a self-invested personal pension.

Residential Mortgages

Although residential mortgages are available on every high street, it is difficult to know which are the best options. With building societies, banks and centralised lenders all active in the market, the choice is wider than ever.

Which type of scheme is the first choice to be made, whether you want a fixed or discounted rate or perhaps a 'cashback'. A fixed rate, where the rate of interest charged is set at outset for a predetermined period, provides stability and security. If however you feel that interest rates are likely to fall, a discounted rate may suit you better. You would then pay interest at a rate lower than the standard variable rate, although this may increase or decrease. With a cashback scheme you pay at the standard rate, without any concessions, but receive a substantial cash sum following completion. This is generally between 3% and 5% of the loan amount. Another factor in the choice of scheme is how long you are likely to remain in the property. Most schemes, whether fixed or discounted, now attract substantial penalties for redeeming early.

The next decision is how the mortgage is to be repaid. This can be on a traditional capital and interest (repayment) basis, or interest-only, linked to a suitable repayment vehicle. This could be a personal equity plan, an endowment policy, or a pension. It is essential that professional advice is taken at this point. In most cases, life assurance will be recommended.

The various costs associated with a new mortgage must be taken into consideration. All purchases of over £60,000 attract stamp duty at 1% of the purchase price. Valuation and survey fees must be paid, and possibly an arrangement fee from the lender, particularly if a fixed rate is chosen. If the mortgage required is over 75% of the valuation, an additional charge known as an indemnity guarantee premium, is usually payable. If the mortgage is 95% of the valuation this could be well over £1,000, so it may be necessary to choose a lender where this could be added to the mortgage.

It is a fact that there are few lenders who really appreciate the requirements of those who do not have standard salaried employment. Whether someone is self-employed, a director of a limited company, or employed on a short term contract, income is likely to fluctuate over the years. Flexible and sympathetic underwriting is often required, particularly if additional funds are to be raised. There are fortunately a number of lenders who will look at an individual's ability to pay rather than just applying standard income multipliers.

A plethora of mortgage payment protection policies have recently been launched by lenders but the small print must be examined carefully. The policies are aimed primarily at employees and so are unlikely to provide adequate protection to the self-employed.

ELEMENT 10 : CLAIMING BENEFIT

As a self employed person you are allowed to seek help from all sources that are there for the employed. This means, contrary to popular mythology, that you are allowed to sign on and get housing benefit if things fall flat and/or hard times come thick and fast. It may be for only a few weeks or months that you need assistance; it may be for a couple of years, but, whenever the problems start to arise, it is essential to deal with them immediately.

What help is available?

Firstly there is the national statutory amount which at present (1996) is £46.50 per week, available to all applicants, subject to meeting statutory requirements.

There is also the availability of support with National Insurance contributions, which are normally credited in full during the period of signing on. Please note that the NI contributions are specifically the stamps that all employed people pay on a weekly or monthly basis. They are different and separate from the NI deductions that are calculated on your annual tax returns. In addition, there are support structures for council tax payments and housing benefits and, where applicable, for child support where not already claimed.

These three areas provide essential support in areas that are often the most worrying in terms of stress and insecurity. To know that they are there allows certain pressures to be lifted at a time when there is so much else to cope with.

If you do not exceed more than 16 hours work a week, you are automatically eligible for benefits. If you work less than 16 hours a week (two working days) whilst you are signed on it will not affect your benefit, but you are obliged to declare the hours that you work (ie. are employed). The amount that you are paid for this work does not affect your right to claim benefit. However if the amount you earn and declare is greater than the weekly benefit (£46.50 at present), then you are not allocated benefit for that particular week. The amount earned by the work does NOT roll over week by week. The amount that constitutes earnings is the net income from the job, thus, if you handle heavy expenses, these do not constitute earnings.

You are able to draw council tax relief immediately you sign on and apply for housing benefits, whether it be mortgage relief or rent paid. If you have a mortgage that was taken out prior to October '95 the new laws about relief payments do not apply.

Full details of all benefits are available from any Social Security office and local DHS offices can supply full details of Housing benefits and Council Tax help.

How long does it take?

Your benefits will be calculated the date you apply and are registered. At present the DHS and Benefits offices take around a week to 10 days to process the applications. Housing benefits can take a little while longer, but everything is backdated to the day that you apply. The important thing to do is apply as soon as possible; be patient with the system and keep a record of names and times of conversations with all those that you deal with.

Mortgage Relief

With every mortgage the interest is generally paid in full. So if you have an endowment mortgage the majority of the monthly payment is met, with a repayment mortgage the interest alone is paid. For the first 16 weeks of benefit, the amount paid towards the monthly rent or mortgage is less than 100%. From the 17th week the interest is paid at 100%. There is a limit to the amount that interest is paid on and at present this figure is £125,000. In either case, an approach to the mortgage company to let them know of the difficulty in maintaining the payments will universally be met with understanding and a sympathetic ear. As long as they can see something coming in, they will be helpful. Even if your mortgage is with your bank, do not be afraid to deal with the relevant department. It does NOT jeopardise your standing or position with the bank.

There are plans to decrease the payments of housing benefits but they apply to those mortgages that were taken out after October '95. The local benefits office will clarify the present rulings.

Exemptions from Social Security Benefits

You will be ineligible to claim for Social Security Benefits if:

- you or your partner work more than 16 hours a week. However this may not affect you being able to get housing support.
- if your savings are over £8,000. If your capital or savings are between £3,000-£8,000 there is a pro rata deduction of £1 for every £250 above £3,000 per week. The amount of savings held by your partner is also considered and included in these amounts.

What to expect when signing on

Make every possible arrangement to be actively looking for work while you are signed on. This means visiting all those contacts you have, looking for job opportunities in the press and sourcing work from every point. Ultimately the term 'actively looking for work' sees the end goal as being in full time employment. A three monthly interview must be attended at your local employment office where you will need to show them that you are "actively looking for work". These meetings are specifically there to help and advise you - show them you are serious in your quest and they will continue to be helpful.

Unit 12 : Digital & Electronic Imaging

INTRODUCTION

The aim of this unit is to make the photographer think carefully about the opportunities offered by new technology, and to consider what its real use is to the photographer and to the rest of the creator community. The possibilities offered by new technology are considered in the context of the rules which apply to the digital environment, particularly the laws of copyright.

The unit will look at how copyright applies to the photographer when licensing digital use of their existing photographs, how the photographer should respect the copyright in other creators' works when working in the digital environment, and how copyright applies to entirely new photographic works created in the digital environment.

ELEMENT 1 : THE IMPACT OF THE NEW TECHNOLOGIES

The 'new' technologies may have been around for some time, but it is only recently that they have had a real impact on professional practice for photographers. Lawyers, creators, media (publisher, producer and broadcaster) and end users (the consumer) have long been anticipating the challenges and the potential of digital and electronic media, but it has taken time for the marketplace for new technologies to develop, and until that market starts to mature it would be foolish, or even dangerous, to establish new rules and practice for trading in that market which have the potential to undermine and radically change systems which have worked well in more traditional areas.

The reference to 'trading' may seem out of place in a publication about photography, but the value of the new media lies not so much in hardware or software, but in content. Content is information; it makes entertainment, it provides education, it makes the new media attractive to the consumer. And whether it takes the form of art, photography, film, video, literature or music, or some compilation of these, content is made up of creative works which are protected by intellectual property (ie. copyright). Ownership of content and the key with which to access it, have tremendous value in the digital environment.

Copyright gives the creator first ownership of copyright and, with that, the right to permit or prohibit reproduction of their work (u1:e1:p11). It provides the photographer with the means of earning their living and protecting their work. In the context of new media, copyright provides the photographer with the key which enables them to trade in access to content, that is, control of their photographs.

A bright new world of opportunities should be opening for the creator community. Instead, both copyright and creator are under renewed attack. Predatory media owners in the traditional broadcast and publishing world are desperate to acquire content, to build up their content assets and, in doing so, deprive photographers and other creators of their copyright, building the 'all rights' culture so often referred to by media lawyers.

New media producers who, in general, have little understanding of the business of licensing, complain that copyright owners are restricting access to their material and that the rules must be changed if the media is to develop to its full potential. The educational and library communities are demanding greater freedom to use copyright material, and last but not least, the anarchic basis on which the Internet itself was established, creates a demand that copyright be abandoned altogether.

So, photographers must deal with commercial asset strippers whilst also resisting pressure for their photographs to become 'public domain'.

ELEMENT 2 : WHAT USE ARE THE NEW TECHNOLOGIES?

There is a great deal of hype about digital technology and what it does. Certainly it has potential, particularly for education, science and medicine, but what does digital technology offer the photographer, and how does this affect their work and their business? Digital technology and use fall most easily into one of three categories:

a) The Tool

In time, digital cameras may replace more traditional equipment, and in the advertising world manual retouching and photocomping are now being replaced by digital retouching and image manipulation. On-line delivery of images from digital camera to advertising agency and on to a digital retouching suite may replace the photolab and delivery van, but it's only the tools which are replaced; the relationship between photographer and equipment, photographer and client, or photographer and supplier, remains unchanged and there should be little or no difference in the rules which apply to these.

b) The Medium or Carrier

At present, most CD-ROMs are little more than books 'printed' on a plastic disk and viewed not on paper, but on computer. Internet as a carrier provides a new means of communication, whether as a new channel for digital 'broadcasting' or for transmitting magazines and newspapers direct to subscribers rather than through the post or retail sale. The Website provides a new advertising medium, for example an annual report and publicity brochure for a national bank. If the carrier has a parallel in the analogue world, then surely the rules of the analogue world can be successfully applied and there is no need for radical change here.

c) Creative Form

Most multimedia products take the form of compilations of other types of creative works, and no new form of creativity is immediately apparent. Of course, this could change. Photography itself was not recognised as a creative form until quite recently, and films (movies that is) were not protected by copyright as cinematographic works until 1956, before that they were treated only as strings of photographs or dramatic works.

The cutting edge of art and photography practice may be in 'computer imaging', but again these can be dealt with in the same way as other artistic works, and the computer merely provides the tool with which to make the work. The concern here is that many of these images take as origination the photographs and works of other creators, reworked and manipulated in a form similar to the collage (u1:e9:p22). When dealing with the digital collage, photographers should remember that, whilst the making of physical collages do not normally involve reproduction, the computer collage does.

Computer generated images are relatively new forms of creativity and are protected quite separately in copyright law. Such works are understood to have no human author and are quite different to artistic works which have been created by the photographer on a computer. The copyright owner of a computer generated work is the person by whom the arrangements necessary for the creation of the work are undertaken and not the creator.

Perhaps in time new forms of creativity will emerge, but at present there is nothing, in legal terms, which falls outside existing categories of creative work.

To summarise: where parallels exist between the analogue and digital, there is no real need for drastic change or abandonment of the rules which already apply. There is, however, a need for some adaptation or extension of those rules.

ELEMENT 3 : WHAT RULES?

The Importance of the Reproduction Right

The main economic right which photographers control through their copyright is the reproduction right. It is important to remember this, because there are other rights, such as broadcasting, distribution and adaptation rights. These apply more specifically to other categories of copyright works; for example, broadcasting directly applies to music, dramatic works and films. But for the photographer, when their work is broadcast in a television programme or included in a film, then it is, first and foremost, reproduced. Adaptation rights apply when a literary work is changed into a dramatic work, for example when a book is rewritten in script form for performance as a play. There is no adaptation right for a photograph or other artistic work, but to adapt a still image of any kind, it must first be reproduced, and the photographer is therefore still in a position to use copyright.

It is constantly asked why there are no definitive rules for licensing photographs for digital use as yet, but in many cases the old rules are still valid and the problem lies, not in defining copyright, but defining what is meant by terms such as 'digital and electronic use' or 'new technology' or 'multimedia'. There are, of course, some areas in which answers have yet to be found and the legal debates continue, whether in the World Intellectual Property Organisation (WIPO), at Government level in the USA, Japan or Europe, or indeed within the publishing and music industries of the UK.

Copyright in Photographic Works in Digital Form

The relevance of the reproduction right may seem academic, but if digital rights are to be successfully defined and clarified for photographers, then the first point is that it is the reproduction right which is most likely to apply for photographs.

In some cases, reproductions may be temporary or transient, for example where an image is transmitted on a network, or where a reproduction of the stored image is a necessary part of displaying the photograph on screen. Transient copies are treated as reproduction under UK law.

The current legislative debate covers issues such as where reproductions arise (eg. on the internet), whether other acts (such as broadcasting or distribution) occur, how reproduction can be controlled or charged for, and whether these should be paid. This section provides a list of the rights relevant to the photographer at present but it also highlights some of the issues which are still unresolved.

One such right is around the 'right to read'. When we buy a book we certainly don't expect to pay separately for the right to read it; but if the text of a book has been stored on computer in a college it will not be accessed by just one person. That single act of storage could make the book available to be read by several hundred students. The author will receive payment for only one digital copy, that is the copy which was licensed and legitimately stored in the computer. Going back a stage further, few copies will be sold in book form, the author will lose the main part of their livelihood and the publisher will be less prepared to invest in such publications. Neither will want to see their publication appearing in digital form. This type of use has a major economic impact on the author and publisher, and the same applies for the photographer. These issues become of even greater importance where commercial audiences, that is the consumer marketplace, is involved, and where works are made available on open networks.

Digital Rights

The first step is to break down digital use of the photograph:

Inputting or storing
To store a photograph in digital form, it must first be copied, normally by scanning the image and storing it in the computer memory.

Screen display
To view an image on a computer screen means making a transient or temporary copy inside the computer which results in the appearance of that image on the screen.

Downloading
Downloading could cover anything from low resolution paper print-outs, akin to photocopies, to copies on floppy or video disk at high resolution and intended as origination for further reproductions, perhaps in traditional print media. It could also mean copying onto another computer disk or onto CD-ROM or equivalent.

Distribution
Distribution is also a right, not one which is generally used when granting licences for photographs, because clearly there is little point in granting reproduction rights to a newspaper publisher if the photographer doesn't also grant the right to distribute the newspapers which include the reproduction. However, in the digital environment, distribution does become relevant.

Generally, distribution applies to copyright works in 'material form'. Material form means physical objects, actual products, such as newspapers or even CD-ROMs. But what about the Internet? There are no physical objects changing hands on the Internet, but there is clearly reproduction and distribution (that is, uses which should be charged for), so there are some new problems to be dealt with. The first is defining the points at which reproduction takes place. The second is who is responsible for clearing and paying for copyright; should it be the inputter of the photograph, the provider of the service in which the photograph is included, or the receiver and end user of the photograph? Distribution and associated issues are currently being reviewed by the international copyright community.

Manipulation
Digital manipulation of a photograph means first making a copy, so reproduction rights apply, and photographers can also use their moral rights for protection. It is possible, however, that other creators of copyright works will also be able to use the adaptation right (u12:e3:p98) and in the future the adaptation right could be extended to cover manipulation of photographs and other artistic works in the digital environment.

It will be some time before these issues are fully resolved, but in the meantime photographers and other creators will want to make their work available for the new media. But how can they do this safely?

ELEMENT 4 : HOW TO LICENCE DIGITAL USE

Knowing what rights are involved doesn't help the photographer to negotiate terms or to grant a licence, unless the photographer is clear about what the user wants to do with the photograph. Photographers should not be afraid to ask, or to insist on detailed explanations when new media producers introduce technical jargon or vague concepts of use.

If the producer, publisher or other client is unclear, then a licence should be granted in the narrowest possible terms, with an agreement to issue further licences and negotiate fresh terms and more fees as and when they become clear on their requirements. For example, a licence could be given to store the photograph and to develop a product or project, but no further rights such as 'production and distribution of 20,000 CD-ROMs' would be granted until the producer is in a position to confirm this requirement.

Photographers should follow the publisher's recommendation for licensing in the digital environment, that is to 'licence narrowly', if they wish to reap the greatest returns from the new media. They should grant only the rights, and limit use, to exactly what is required now, and not at some unspecified date in the future. Photographers should not agree to terms which include 'all electronic rights'. If the product is successful, then the producer can alway return for further grants of rights.

So what types of use are likely to arise? Many will be similar to those with which photographers are already familiar, it may just take a little longer to get the position absolutely clear with the client.

For example, a national gallery may wish to show a photograph on screens or workstations to thousands of visitors to the gallery, but will have only one hard disk from which the images are networked to the computer workstations. To licence storage on the single hard disk would not cover the mass use of the work, and fees negotiated for that single storage would not provide sufficient recompense for the photographer.

On the other hand, a photographer may be invited to contribute a single image to an interactive multimedia programme containing hundreds of other works which will be available on hundreds of thousands of CD-ROMs worldwide; each of these discs will be sold only to the consumer market for access in private by a single individual. This type of use is more akin to book sales, but the photographer should consider that their contribution is only one of many hundreds or thousands and insistence on a high fee will make inclusion of the photograph uneconomical for the producer.

The photographer must take into account what is fair to the client as well as what is reasonable for themselves.

The Licence for Digital Use

Once the photographer knows what usage is involved and what rights apply, and has negotiated a fee, it is time to negotiate other essential terms and to issue a licence as they would for any other type of use.

Photographers are referred to the Advertising Licence form (*ill 3:p109*) and listed below are some of the key points to be covered when licensing digital or electronic use

- Publisher/Producer's Name;
- Any other participants (most projects have more than one party involved);
- Title or working title for the project;
- Title of work to be used, ie. title of the photograph or a clear description of it;
- Confirmation of copyright byline or credit to be included;
- Type of use. This always includes storing the work in digital form and then whatever other type of use is required eg. Production Licence for Retail Sale of a CD-ROM;
- Short description of the project. This helps clarify the nature of the product;
- Format/Platform: firstly the format on which the Master is being produced, eg. Syquest cartridge, then the final format, eg. CD-ROM. Define this as narrowly as possible;
- Quantity. How many masters and back up copies will there be? How many CD-ROM's do they want to produce? How many workstations will the data be accessible on?;
- Image Quality. Some artists want high quality, some want low, others will allow high on-screen but want very low for paper print-outs. You may also wish to confirm the quality at which the image can be stored;
- Territory/Language. Increasingly difficult to give anything less than worldwide, but useful if the product is only being licensed for use at a single site;
- Completion/Publication Date;
- Term of the Licence.

Some of the following may also be worth including:

- Exclusion of rental and lending rights;
- Prohibition of inclusion in a cable or on-line service;
- Procedure for approval;
- Prohibition on public display (unless this is specifically granted);
- Inclusion of copy protection mechanisms;
- Prohibition on printing out or other hard copies (unless this is specifically granted);
- Express terms relating to transfers of copies of photographs in electronic form (this relates to Section 56 of the 1988 Copyright Act);
- Prohibition on manipulation (unless this has been agreed);
- Reasonable quality of reproduction;
- Assertion of, and respect for, moral rights;
- No reproduction of the work in any packaging or advertising (unless this is part of a separate licensing deal);
- Number of complementary copies of CD-ROM for the photographer.

ELEMENT 5 : MORAL RIGHTS IN THE DIGITAL ENVIRONMENT

Moral Rights apply in the digital environment as they do in traditional media. The main difficulty, as with traditional media, is in enforcing them, and it is recommended that contractual conditions are included in the terms of any licence granted which cover moral rights.

Moral Rights have increased significance in this area because of the ease with which photographs and other copyright works can be inputted, copied and transmitted via computer systems and computer networks.

Paternity Right (u2:e2:p27)

With so many perfect digital copies in circulation, the photographer would, no doubt, prefer to be associated with their photograph wherever it appears. And surely the provenance of a photograph would be of general interest to the public who would like to know who created the original photograph, particularly if there are to be millions of adaptations and manipulations. The photograph could carry its pedigree so that those with an interest, such as academics, critics and creators, would know who contributed what, why and at what stage.

The Integrity Right (u2:e2:p28)
This is the right to prevent derogatory treatment, to preserve the integrity of a photograph. Moral rights have always been personal rights of the creator, and tend to be associated with their ego. But there is a new issue at stake on the Internet and that is public interest; interest in knowing whether a work is original, not just in a historic or aesthetic sense, but in terms of news and current affairs. The public are interested in whether the photographs are original or whether they are manipulated, for example to provide a newspaper proprietor or editor's view of the world. Of course, retouching and photocomposites have always been available, but the ease with which digital manipulation can be carried out and the difficulty of detecting such changes, make it difficult to know which was the original image. In the past, the photographer was normally involved, or at least was aware of such manipulations, but with the advent of digital cameras which transmit images across continents direct to the picture desk, the photographer may not be aware that changes have been made until after the photograph has been published.

These issues are fundamental and should be debated by students who will be the next generation of photographers and image makers, and who will have to work with these ethical dilemmas. The current generation of photographers is getting to grips with them, and, within the professional organisations, codes of practice and ethics for image manipulation are now being devised; but it is the next generation of photographers who must put them into practice.

ELEMENT 6 : OTHER DIGITAL ISSUES

Copyright in the Digital Version of a Photograph

Some multimedia producers and some stock agencies are claiming there is a separate copyright in the digital version of a photograph (u1:e9:p28). The terms of the representation or acquisition agreement they offer photographers makes it clear that, whilst the photographer keeps the copyright in the photograph, they (the producer or agency) have created a new copyright which they own by the act of scanning and storing the photograph.

No such separate copyright exists in either UK or other European legislation and its status in the USA is also very doubtful.

Students and photographers dealing with companies making such claims are advised to contact the professional organisations for more information and advice.

Appropriation of other Artistic Works

As has already been mentioned, making a photographic collage using works or parts of works by cutting or clipping images from publications is not in itself illegal. It is not until that collage is copied or reproduced, for example in a magazine or newspaper, that an infringement of copyright will exist in that unlicensed copy. In addition, the moral rights (see Unit 2) of the original photographers may have been breached.

However, a similar collage produced on computer is different because the photographs must be scanned and stored in the computer, and to make them available to others they must be displayed on screen or downloaded in some form (u12:e2c:p98), and this means the original works are reproduced in the making of the collage.

Quite apart from the fact that most reproductions of a photograph require the photographer's prior permission, photographers, and indeed other artists, are particularly careful about how and when their works become available in the digital environment and, quite reasonably, they wish to keep control of digitisation in their own hands. Students who scan and manipulate the works of other artists and photographers should be aware of this, and permission should always be sought first.

Copyright in Underlying Works

Where a copyright work is included in another copyright work, for example, part of a stock photograph is used to incorporate a key feature into another photograph for advertising purposes, then this is known as an 'underlying work'.

Where permission is given for the inclusion of one photograph in another artistic work, if sufficient creative input makes the second image an original work in its own right, then a separate copyright owned by the second creator, and not the original photographer, will apply to that new photograph. However, that does not affect the copyright protection afforded to the underlying photograph, which remains with the first photographer and which must be respected; that is, any reproduction of the second image must carry the approval of the first photographer.

Confidentiality and Privacy

Confidentiality and privacy are issues which have been dealt with in earlier units, and for most photographers they apply in the digital environment as elsewhere. However, for those photographers working in the medical and forensic sectors they are issues of major importance. Images which, until now, have been held in collections in some physical form, for example, slides for teaching purposes, are rapidly being digitised and stored in databases around the country. Increasingly those databases are being linked together and may soon be accessed widely on networks. Patients who had no objections to use of the images for training doctors in a teaching hospital, might feel differently if the images can be openly accessed through the Internet. Patient confidentiality is an important subject for debate in this sector of photography.

ELEMENT 7 : PROTECTING PHOTOGRAPHS ON THE INTERNET

There is no definitive guide to protecting photographs on the Internet. On the whole, full protection is just not possible at present, so if in doubt, don't!

The difficulties of defining reproduction and distribution on networks has already been mentioned, along with the problems of preventing manipulation. It is virtually impossible to control unlicensed use and re-use of works and, where reproductions are licensed, it is not easy to measure use and thus establish reasonable levels of fees. For these reasons, many artists are reluctant to permit their work to be used on open networks at present.

However, other artists and photographers see the Internet as an opportunity to get further exposure for their work. If approached by an on-line service provider wanting to include photographs, the photographer should first find out more about the service. How is the service paid for - is the photographer expected to pay for the privilege of being included or will subscribers pay for access to the images? What is the aim of the service - is it a virtual gallery promoting visits to a more traditional gallery, or is it a publicly funded artists' database aimed at promoting work opportunities for contributing photographers?

If the photographer feels it is a worthwhile opportunity, then they should consider carefully which of their works should be included; perhaps those which do not have a great deal of value in reproduction terms, or a work created especially for the network, inviting user interaction. It is an opportunity to experiment, but the photographer should ensure it doesn't cost, either financially or by devaluing and debasing their works in some other way.

COMMISSION ESTIMATE

The Agency :

Photographer's Name :
Agent/Rep :
Photographer's Ref. No. :
Date :
Art order No :

The Advertiser :

Product :

Job Description :

Media use/period of use/territory : ☐ **Right to a Credit**

Exclusivity period : Term of the licence plus ____________ years (Subject to clause 5 overleaf)

Fees :

Commission fee ____________________

Pre/post production fee ____________________

Other (specifiy) ____________________

Base Usage Rate ____________________

Total fees ____________________

Expenses :

Film, Processing & Polaroid ____________________

Prints ____________________

Location services ____________________

Travel ____________________

Subsistence ____________________

Production co-ordination/Assistants ____________________

Stylist ____________________

Make-up/Hair ____________________

Set build ____________________

Props/Wardrobe ____________________

Studio hire ____________________

Equipment hire ____________________

Models/Casting (billed direct?) ____________________

Rush charges/Overtime ____________________

Special insurance ____________________

Messenger/Delivery ____________________

Miscellaneous ____________________

____

____

Total Expenses ____________________

ESTIMATE TOTAL (exc. VAT) ____________________

Contingency ____________ % of ESTIMATE TOTAL (exc. VAT) ____________________

Advance required before shoot commencement (exc. VAT) ____________________

THIS COMMISSION IS SUBJECT TO ALL TERMS AND CONDITIONS ABOVE AND OVERLEAF.
UNDER CLAUSE 4 OVERLEAF, NO USE MY BE MADE OF THE PHOTOGRAPHS UNTIL THE INVOICE IS PAID IN FULL

ILLUSTRATION I

TERMS AND CONDITIONS

1. DEFINITIONS
For the purpose of this agreement "the Agency' and 'the Advertiser' shall where the context so admits include their respective assignees, sub-licensees and successors in title. In cases where the Photographer's client is a direct client (i.e. with no agency or intermediary), all references in this agreement to both 'the Agency' and 'the Advertiser' shall be interpreted as references to the Photographer's client. 'Photographs' means all photographic material furnished by the Photographer, whether transparencies, negatives, prints or any other type of physical or electronic material.

2. COPYRIGHT
The entire copyright in the Photographs is retained by the Photographer at all times throughout the world.

3. OWNERSHIP OF MATERIALS
Title to all Photographs remains the property of the Photographer. When the Licence to Use the material has expired the Photographs must be returned to the Photographer in good condition within 30 days.

4. USE
The Licence to Use comes into effect from the date of payment of the relevant invoice(s). No use may be made of the Photographs before payment in full of the relevant invoice(s) without the Photographer's express permission. Any permission which may be given for prior use will automatically be revoked if full payment is not made by the due date or if the Agency is put into receivership or liquidation. The Licence only applies to the advertiser and product as stated on the front of the form and its benefit shall not be assigned to any third party without the Photographer's permission. Accordingly, even where any form of 'all media' Licence is granted, the photographer's permission must be obtained before any use of the Photographs for other purposes eg use in relation to another product or sublicensing through a photolibrary. Permission to use the Photographs for purposes outside the terms of the Licence will normally be granted upon payment of a further fee, which must be mutually agreed (and paid in full) before such further use. Unless otherwise agreed in writing, all further Licences in respect of the Photographs will be subject to these terms and conditions.

5. EXCLUSIVITY
The Agency and Advertiser will be authorised to publish the Photographs to the exclusion of all other persons including the Photographer. However, the Photographer retains the right in all cases to use the Photographs in any manner at any time and in any part of the world for the purposes of advertising or otherwise promoting his/her work. After the exclusivity period indicated in the Licence to Use the Photographer shall be entitled to use the Photographs for any purposes.

6. CLIENT CONFIDENTIALITY
The photographer will keep confidential and will not disclose to any third parties or make use of material or information communicated to him/her in confidence for the purposes of the photography, save as may be reasonably necessary to enable the Photographer to carry out his/her obligations in relation to the commission.

7. INDEMNITY
The Photographer agrees to indemnify the Agency and the Advertiser against all expenses, damages, claims and legal costs arising out of any failure by the Photographer to obtain any clearances for which he/she was responsible in respect of third party copyright works, trade marks, designs or other intellectual property. The Photographer shall only be responsible for obtaining such clearances if this has been expressly agreed before the shoot. In all other cases the Agency shall be responsible for obtaining such clearances and will indemnify the Photographer against all expenses, damages, claims and legal costs arising out of any failure to obtain such clearances.

8. PAYMENT
Payment by the Agency will be expected for the commissioned work within 30 days of the issue of the relevant invoice. If the invoice is not paid, in full, within 30 days The Photographer reserves the right to charge interest at the rate prescribed by the Late Payment of Commercial Debt (Interest) Act 1998 from the date payment was due until the date payment is made.

9. EXPENSES
Where extra expenses or time are incurred by the Photographer as a result of alterations to the original brief by the Agency or the Advertiser, or otherwise at their request, the Agency shall give approval to and be liable to pay such extra expenses or fees at the Photographer's normal rate to the Photographer in addition to the expenses shown overleaf as having been agreed or estimated.

10. REJECTION
Unless a rejection fee has been agreed in advance, there is no right to reject on the basis of style or composition.

11. CANCELLATION & POSTPONEMENT
A booking is considered firm as from the date of confirmation and accordingly the Photographer will, at his/her discretion, charge a fee for cancellation or postponement.

12. RIGHT TO A CREDIT
If the box on the estimate and the licence marked 'Right to a Credit' has been ticked the Photographer's name will be printed on or in reasonable proximity to all published reproductions of the Photograph(s). By ticking the box overleaf the Photographer also asserts his/her statutory right to be identified in the circumstances set out in Sections 77-79 of the Copyright, Designs and Patents Act 1988 or any amendment or re-enactment thereof.

13. ELECTRONIC STORAGE
Save for the purposes of reproduction for the licensed use(s), the Photographs may not be stored in any form of electronic medium without the written permission of the Photographer. Manipulation of the image or use of only a portion of the image may only take place with the permission of the Photographer.

14. APPLICABLE LAW
This agreement shall be governed by the laws of England, Wales and Scotland.

15. VARIATION
These Terms and Conditions shall not be varied except by agreement in writing.

NOTE : For more information on the commissioning of advertising photography refer to the interim guidelines produced by the Association of Photographers.

COMMISSION INVOICE

The Agency :	Photographer's Name :
	Agent/Rep :
	Photographer's Ref. No. :
	Date :
	Art order No :
The Advertiser :	Product :

Job Description :

Media use/period of use/territory :

(for fill details see attached 'Licence to Use' No. __________)

Fees :

Commission fee	____________	
Pre/post production fee	____________	
Other (specifiy)	____________	
Base Usage Rate ____________		
	Total fees	____________

Expenses :

Film, Processing & Polaroid	____________	
Prints	____________	
Location services	____________	
Travel	____________	
Subsistence	____________	
Production co-ordination/Assistants	____________	
Stylist	____________	
Make-up/Hair	____________	
Set build	____________	
Props/Wardrobe	____________	
Studio hire	____________	
Equipment hire	____________	
Models/Casting (billed direct?)	____________	
Rush charges/Overtime	____________	
Special insurance	____________	
Messenger/Delivery	____________	
Miscellaneous	____________	
	Total Expenses	____________

Sub-total	____________
VAT	____________
TOTAL COST	____________
Less Advance Paid	____________
TOTAL AMOUNT DUE	____________

THIS COMMISSION IS SUBJECT TO ALL TERMS AND CONDITIONS ABOVE AND OVERLEAF.
UNDER CLAUSE 4 OVERLEAF, NO USE MY BE MADE OF THE PHOTOGRAPHS UNTIL THE INVOICE IS PAID IN FULL

ILLUSTRATION 2

TERMS AND CONDITIONS

1. DEFINITIONS

For the purpose of this agreement "the Agency' and 'the Advertiser' shall where the context so admits include their respective assignees, sub-licensees and successors in title. In cases where the Photographer's client is a direct client (i.e. with no agency or intermediary), all references in this agreement to both 'the Agency' and 'the Advertiser' shall be interpreted as references to the Photographer's client. 'Photographs' means all photographic material furnished by the Photographer, whether transparencies, negatives, prints or any other type of physical or electronic material.

2. COPYRIGHT

The entire copyright in the Photographs is retained by the Photographer at all times throughout the world.

3. OWNERSHIP OF MATERIALS

Title to all Photographs remains the property of the Photographer. When the Licence to Use the material has expired the Photographs must be returned to the Photographer in good condition within 30 days.

4. USE

The Licence to Use comes into effect from the date of payment of the relevant invoice(s). No use may be made of the Photographs before payment in full of the relevant invoice(s) without the Photographer's express permission. Any permission which may be given for prior use will automatically be revoked if full payment is not made by the due date or if the Agency is put into receivership or liquidation. The Licence only applies to the advertiser and product as stated on the front of the form and its benefit shall not be assigned to any third party without the Photographer's permission. Accordingly, even where any form of 'all media' Licence is granted, the photographer's permission must be obtained before any use of the Photographs for other purposes eg use in relation to another product or sublicensing through a photolibrary. Permission to use the Photographs for purposes outside the terms of the Licence will normally be granted upon payment of a further fee, which must be mutually agreed (and paid in full) before such further use. Unless otherwise agreed in writing, all further Licences in respect of the Photographs will be subject to these terms and conditions.

5. EXCLUSIVITY

The Agency and Advertiser will be authorised to publish the Photographs to the exclusion of all other persons including the Photographer. However, the Photographer retains the right in all cases to use the Photographs in any manner at any time and in any part of the world for the purposes of advertising or otherwise promoting his/her work. After the exclusivity period indicated in the Licence to Use the Photographer shall be entitled to use the Photographs for any purposes.

6. CLIENT CONFIDENTIALITY

The photographer will keep confidential and will not disclose to any third parties or make use of material or information communicated to him/her in confidence for the purposes of the photography, save as may be reasonably necessary to enable the Photographer to carry out his/her obligations in relation to the commission.

7. INDEMNITY

The Photographer agrees to indemnify the Agency and the Advertiser against all expenses, damages, claims and legal costs arising out of any failure by the Photographer to obtain any clearances for which he/she was responsible in respect of third party copyright works, trade marks, designs or other intellectual property. The Photographer shall only be responsible for obtaining such clearances if this has been expressly agreed before the shoot. In all other cases the Agency shall be responsible for obtaining such clearances and will indemnify the Photographer against all expenses, damages, claims and legal costs arising out of any failure to obtain such clearances.

8. PAYMENT

Payment by the Agency will be expected for the commissioned work within 30 days of the issue of the relevant invoice. If the invoice is not paid, in full, within 30 days The Photographer reserves the right to charge interest at the rate prescribed by the Late Payment of Commercial Debt (Interest) Act 1998 from the date payment was due until the date payment is made.

9. EXPENSES

Where extra expenses or time are incurred by the Photographer as a result of alterations to the original brief by the Agency or the Advertiser, or otherwise at their request, the Agency shall give approval to and be liable to pay such extra expenses or fees at the Photographer's normal rate to the Photographer in addition to the expenses shown overleaf as having been agreed or estimated.

10. REJECTION

Unless a rejection fee has been agreed in advance, there is no right to reject on the basis of style or composition.

11. CANCELLATION & POSTPONEMENT

A booking is considered firm as from the date of confirmation and accordingly the Photographer will, at his/her discretion, charge a fee for cancellation or postponement.

12. RIGHT TO A CREDIT

If the box on the estimate and the licence marked 'Right to a Credit' has been ticked the Photographer's name will be printed on or in reasonable proximity to all published reproductions of the Photograph(s). By ticking the box overleaf the Photographer also asserts his/her statutory right to be identified in the circumstances set out in Sections 77-79 of the Copyright, Designs and Patents Act 1988 or any amendment or re-enactment thereof.

13. ELECTRONIC STORAGE

Save for the purposes of reproduction for the licensed use(s), the Photographs may not be stored in any form of electronic medium without the written permission of the Photographer. Manipulation of the image or use of only a portion of the image may only take place with the permission of the Photographer.

14. APPLICABLE LAW

This agreement shall be governed by the laws of England, Wales and Scotland.

15. VARIATION

These Terms and Conditions shall not be varied except by agreement in writing.

NOTE : For more information on the commissioning of advertising photography refer to the interim guidelines produced by the Association of Photographers.

LICENCE TO USE

Granted to (The Agency) :

Photographer's Name :
Agent/Rep :
Photographer's Ref. No. :
Date :
Art order No :

The Advertiser :

Product :

Description of photograph/s covered by the licence:

Terms of the licence :

Media Use

- ☐ Artist reference
- ☐ Brochure
- ☐ Catalogue
- ☐ Inserts
- ☐ Magazine consumer
- ☐ Magazine trade
- ☐ National press
- ☐ Packaging
- ☐ Point of sale
- ☐ Poster (less than 10sq metres)
- ☐ Poster (more than 10sq metres)
- ☐ Television/Cinema
- ☐ Test
- ☐ Other (specify) : ______________________

Territory :

- ☐ UK
- ☐ Single EC Country
- ☐ Continental Europe
- ☐ USA
- ☐ English language areas
- ☐ Worldwide
- ☐ Other (secify) : ______________________

Time Period

- ☐ One year
- ☐ Two years
- ☐ Other (specify) : ______________________

Right to a credit ☐

Exclusivity Clause

I confirm that subject to clause 5 overleaf I shall not publish or supply the material to any other person for publication during the term of the licence plus _______ years, without the express permission of the Agency or the Advertiser.

I confirm that the Agency and the Advertiser are hereby licensed to reproduce and publish the Photographs, for the above purposes, territories and time period, on the terms and conditions set out overleaf.

Under clause 4 overleaf, no use my be made of the Photographs until the invoice has been paid in full.

Signed : ______________________________________ Date : ____________________

ILLUSTRATION 3

TERMS AND CONDITIONS

1. DEFINITIONS
For the purpose of this agreement "the Agency' and 'the Advertiser' shall where the context so admits include their respective assignees, sub-licensees and successors in title. In cases where the Photographer's client is a direct client (i.e. with no agency or intermediary), all references in this agreement to both 'the Agency' and 'the Advertiser' shall be interpreted as references to the Photographer's client. 'Photographs' means all photographic material furnished by the Photographer, whether transparencies, negatives, prints or any other type of physical or electronic material.

2. COPYRIGHT
The entire copyright in the Photographs is retained by the Photographer at all times throughout the world.

3. OWNERSHIP OF MATERIALS
Title to all Photographs remains the property of the Photographer. When the Licence to Use the material has expired the Photographs must be returned to the Photographer in good condition within 30 days.

4. USE
The Licence to Use comes into effect from the date of payment of the relevant invoice(s). No use may be made of the Photographs before payment in full of the relevant invoice(s) without the Photographer's express permission. Any permission which may be given for prior use will automatically be revoked if full payment is not made by the due date or if the Agency is put into receivership or liquidation. The Licence only applies to the advertiser and product as stated on the front of the form and its benefit shall not be assigned to any third party without the Photographer's permission. Accordingly, even where any form of 'all media' Licence is granted, the photographer's permission must be obtained before any use of the Photographs for other purposes eg use in relation to another product or sublicensing through a photolibrary. Permission to use the Photographs for purposes outside the terms of the Licence will normally be granted upon payment of a further fee, which must be mutually agreed (and paid in full) before such further use. Unless otherwise agreed in writing, all further Licences in respect of the Photographs will be subject to these terms and conditions.

5. EXCLUSIVITY
The Agency and Advertiser will be authorised to publish the Photographs to the exclusion of all other persons including the Photographer. However, the Photographer retains the right in all cases to use the Photographs in any manner at any time and in any part of the world for the purposes of advertising or otherwise promoting his/her work. After the exclusivity period indicated in the Licence to Use the Photographer shall be entitled to use the Photographs for any purposes.

6. CLIENT CONFIDENTIALITY
The photographer will keep confidential and will not disclose to any third parties or make use of material or information communicated to him/her in confidence for the purposes of the photography, save as may be reasonably necessary to enable the Photographer to carry out his/her obligations in relation to the commission.

7. INDEMNITY
The Photographer agrees to indemnify the Agency and the Advertiser against all expenses, damages, claims and legal costs arising out of any failure by the Photographer to obtain any clearances for which he/she was responsible in respect of third party copyright works, trade marks, designs or other intellectual property. The Photographer shall only be responsible for obtaining such clearances if this has been expressly agreed before the shoot. In all other cases the Agency shall be responsible for obtaining such clearances and will indemnify the Photographer against all expenses, damages, claims and legal costs arising out of any failure to obtain such clearances.

8. PAYMENT
Payment by the Agency will be expected for the commissioned work within 30 days of the issue of the relevant invoice. If the invoice is not paid, in full, within 30 days The Photographer reserves the right to charge interest at the rate prescribed by the Late Payment of Commercial Debt (Interest) Act 1998 from the date payment was due until the date payment is made.

9. EXPENSES
Where extra expenses or time are incurred by the Photographer as a result of alterations to the original brief by the Agency or the Advertiser, or otherwise at their request, the Agency shall give approval to and be liable to pay such extra expenses or fees at the Photographer's normal rate to the Photographer in addition to the expenses shown overleaf as having been agreed or estimated.

10. REJECTION
Unless a rejection fee has been agreed in advance, there is no right to reject on the basis of style or composition.

11. CANCELLATION & POSTPONEMENT
A booking is considered firm as from the date of confirmation and accordingly the Photographer will, at his/her discretion, charge a fee for cancellation or postponement.

12. RIGHT TO A CREDIT
If the box on the estimate and the licence marked 'Right to a Credit' has been ticked the Photographer's name will be printed on or in reasonable proximity to all published reproductions of the Photograph(s). By ticking the box overleaf the Photographer also asserts his/her statutory right to be identified in the circumstances set out in Sections 77-79 of the Copyright, Designs and Patents Act 1988 or any amendment or re-enactment thereof.

13. ELECTRONIC STORAGE
Save for the purposes of reproduction for the licensed use(s), the Photographs may not be stored in any form of electronic medium without the written permission of the Photographer. Manipulation of the image or use of only a portion of the image may only take place with the permission of the Photographer.

14. APPLICABLE LAW
This agreement shall be governed by the laws of England, Wales and Scotland.

15. VARIATION
These Terms and Conditions shall not be varied except by agreement in writing.

NOTE : For more information on the commissioning of advertising photography refer to the interim guidelines produced by the Association of Photographers.

ASSISTING PHOTOGRAPHER'S INVOICE **No.** 001

Date :

Ref No. :

Photographer :

Address :

Client/Job Reference :

Fee for Photographic Services :

Job Date/s:

Total Fee ______________

Expenses (specify) :

Total Expenses ______________

Subtotal ______________

VAT ______________

TOTAL AMOUNT DUE ______________

Payable to :

Assisting Photographer :

Address :

Schedule D No. :

VAT Reg. No. :

Payment due on completion of shoot subject to guidelines issued by The Association of Photographers Ltd

ILLUSTRATION 4

Delivery Note

This delivery note does not constitute a right to use
PLEASE KEEP ON FILE

These pictures have been sent on loan. Discrepancies should be advised immediately. Pictures must be returned, or reproduction rights ordered, by the Date for Return to avoid rental fees (see clause 10). Precise reproduction rights and relevant fees for each usage must be agreed before any use is made of the pictures. Please get in touch with us if you desire a reasonable extension of the Date for Return.

Client

Address

Contact

Telephone

Delivery note number

Date

Date for Return

Service £ is separately invoiced

Method of despatch

PLEASE READ OUR TERMS AND CONDITIONS OVERLEAF

Rights to store, transmit or reproduce these images in any electronic form must be negotiated separately

Total Number of Transparencies

Total Number of Prints

Please sign and return one copy to acknowledge safe receipt.

Signature . . . .

Date . . . .

Loss or damage of an original (see 7b over) £

Loss or damage of a print (see 7b over) £

Loss or damage of a duplicate (see 7b over) £

Loss or damage of a specified loan (see 7b over) £

Reproduction without a credit % extra (14a over)

Rental fee per week, per picture (see 10 over) £

Cost of mount replacement (see 8 over) £

Layout fee if security seal is broken £

THE PICTURES LISTED ABOVE HAVE BEEN DELIVERED AT THE CLIENTS REQUEST

1. Any client who has not previously dealt with the Supplier on the terms and conditions set out overleaf and who does not wish to accept such terms and conditions must return all the pictures immediately, properly packed, by any means affording proof of delivery and insured to the relevant level of compensation cover. The client shall be deemed to have accepted the supplier's terms and conditions if all the pictures are not returned within three days of their receipt by the client in the UK or seven days of their receipt overseas.
2. Any client who has previously dealt with the Supplier on the terms and conditions set out overleaf will be deemed to have accepted them by virtue of having made the request for the pictures referred to above.

TERMS AND CONDITIONS OF SUBMISSION AND REPRODUCTION OF PICTURES

1. In this Agreement the terms (a) PICTURE includes a photograph, transparency, negative, design, artwork, painting, montage, drawing, engraving, or any other item which may be offered for the purposes of reproduction; (b) REPRODUCTION includes any form of publication or copying of the whole or part of any picture, altered or not, whether by printing, photography, slide projection (whether or not to an audience), xerography, artist's reference, artist's illustration, layout or presentation, electroni or mechanical reproduction or storage by any other means; (c) DATE FOR RETURN is the date by which the pictures must be returned as specified on the delivery not If no date is specified, the Date for Return shall be four weeks from the date of the delivery note or if an invoice is rendered for reproduction rights, 12 weeks from the date of such invoice.

2. No variation of terms or conditions set out herein shall be effective unless agreed in writing by both parties.

3. Pictures are supplied on LOAN and no property or copyright in any pictures shall pass to the Client whether on its submission or on the Supplier's grant of reproduction rights in respect thereof.

4. A non refundable service fee to cover administrative costs and despatch of pictures is payable by the Client on each submission and resubmission of pictures whether c not reproduction rights are required or granted. The Client shall pay for courier, express or any other special delivery arrangement requested.

5. (a) Reproduction rights (if and when granted) are strictly limited to the use, period of time and territory specified on the Supplier's invoice and unless otherwise agreed in writing relate to a single publication in a single size with text (if any) in one language only.

   (b) Reproduction rights are not granted exclusively to the Client except when specified on the invoice.

   (c) Reproduction rights granted are personal to the Client and may not be assigned, nor may any picture submitted to the Client be loaned or transferred to third parties save for the purpose of the exercise by the Client of such reproduction rights.

   (d) Any reproduction rights granted are by way of licence and no partial or other assignment of copyright shall be implied.

6. The Supplier's delivery note will list all the pictures delivered to the Client, which shall be presumed to have been received in good condition, unless within 3 days of receipt the Supplier receives notification of any discrepancy or damage.

7. (a) Risk in and responsibility for pictures passes to the Client from the time they are received until their safe return. The Client shall immediately inform the Supplie in writing of any known loss or misuse of, or damage to the pictures while in the Client's possession or that of any third party. If a picture is not returned within 12 week of the date for return, the Supplier may in its sole discretion presume it to be lost.

   (b) The Client shall be liable to pay compensation to the Supplier in respect of each picture lost or damaged (see over). The loss or damage of colour or monotone prints or duplicate transparencies for which there are available originals shall also be the subject of compensation, but at a different level (see over). A Supplier may als specify in writing at the time of the loan a different compensation figure for loss or serious damage to certain pictures (see over). Payment of compensation does not gi rise to any rights in any picture. These figures have been assessed by the Supplier and are a genuine pre-estimate of the loss which would be suffered if such a picture were to be lost or damaged. The Client is urged to take out insurance to cover the total value of the pictures delivered.

   (c) A picture subsequently found must be returned immediately. If it is undamaged the Client will be credited with the compensation paid less a rental fee (under Clause 10) from the date the compensation is claimed to the date the picture is returned, such credit being at least 20% of the compensation paid.

8. Any picture returned without its mount or with its caption or other mount data missing or defaced, may incur a replacement charge (see over).

9. The Client must return every picture to the Supplier by its date for return by any method affording proof of delivery and insured to the relevant level of compensation cover. Adequate protection must be given to pictures in transit. A delivery note listing and totalling the returned pictures must be enclosed, and an advice in writing wi this same information sent by separate post.

10. Unless otherwise agreed each picture may be held by the Client rental free until its Date for Return and thereafter the Client shall be liable to pay a rental fee (see ove per picture per week or part thereof pending its return. Payment of the rental fee does not entitle the Client to retain the picture after the Date for Return.

11. (a) Until the Supplier has invoiced the reproduction fee neither party is committed to grant or to acquire any reproduction rights in any picture. After a fee has beer agreed and an invoice issued there is a firm and binding contract whereby the Supplier is committed to grant reproduction rights and the Client to acquire them. If after such invoicing but before payment, the Client requests cancellation of the reproduction rights the Supplier may in its discretion cancel subject to the Client paying a cancellation fee.

   (b) The Client's right to reproduce a picture arises only when the Supplier's invoice relating to the grant of such right is fully paid. Any reproduction before paymen of the invoice constitutes an infringement of rights and a breach of this Agreement entitling the Supplier to rescind the Agreement and rendering the Client liable for the payment of damages.

   (c) The Client agrees to indemnify the Supplier in respect of any claims or damages or any loss or costs arising in any manner from the reproduction without prop reproduction rights of any picture supplied to the Client by the Supplier.

12. (a) The Supplier's invoice shall be paid within 30 days of issue save in the case of newspaper, periodical and broadcasting clients where payment shall be made r later than the end of the calendar month immediately succeeding publication or use.

   (b) If payment is not made in accordance with (a) above then the Supplier may rescind this Agreement and recover damages, or, at its option, may charge interest on the overdue amount at 2% per month on the outstanding balance.

13. On the Client's death or bankruptcy or (if the Client is a Company) in the event of a Resolution, Petition or Order for winding-up being made against it, or if a Receiver appointed, the Supplier may at any time thereafter inspect any records, accounts and books relating to the reproduction of the Supplier's pictures to ensure that the pictures are being used only in accordance with the reproduction rights granted to the Client.

14. (a) Unless otherwise agreed in writing, if any picture reproduced by the Client omits the copyright notice or credit line specified by the Supplier the reproduction fe payable by the Client shall be subject to an increase (see over).

   (b) The Author has asserted his right to a credit in accordance with sections 77 and 78 Copyright, Designs and Patents Act 1988.

15. (a) Electronic use, storage or transmission of images is forbidden without the express written permission of the supplier

   (b) The client will provide any information reasonably requested regarding anti-piracy measures.

16. Pictures shall not be copied, on-loaned or otherwise disposed of and no use whatsoever shall be made of them by the client without prior written consent of the supplie nor shall the image be altered or manipulated, added to, or have any part deleted without the prior written consent of the supplier.

17. In the case of printed publications, two copies of the relevant pages containing any picture supplied are to be furnished to the Supplier by the client free of charge with two weeks. In other media evidence of use must be made available if requested.

18. While the Supplier takes all reasonable care in the performance of this Agreement generally, the Supplier shall not be liable for any loss or damage suffered by the Cli or by any third party arising from use or reproduction of any picture or its caption.

19. It is the Client who must satisfy himself that all necessary rights, model releases or consents which may be required for reproduction, are obtained and it is acknowledged that the Supplier gives no warranty or undertaking that any such rights, releases or consents are or will be obtained whether in relation to the use of names, people, trade marks, registered or copyright designs or works of art depicted in any picture. In the event that the picture is used or reproduced by or with the authority of the Client then the Client shall indemnify the Supplier against any loss, damage, proceedings or costs where such rights, releases or consents have not be obtained.

20. This agreement shall be subject to and construed according to English law and the parties agree to accept the exclusive jurisdiction of the Courts of England.

STANDARD RELEASE FORM

Photographer: ______________________________ Agency/Client: ______________________________

Model/s: ______________________________ Art Order No.: ______________________________

Product: ______________________________ Brand Name: ______________________________

Date/s: ______________________________ Hours Worked: ______________________________

For valuable consideration received *I/we hereby grant the *photographer/agency/client, and any licensees or assignees, the absolute right to use the photograph(s) and any other reproductions or adaptions, from the above mentioned photographic shoot, but only for the product or brand name specified above, solely and exclusively for:

Media

- ☐ Advertising - national press
- ☐ Advertising - trade press
- ☐ Editorial - consumer press
- ☐ Editorial - trade press
- ☐ Editorial - national press
- ☐ Catalogue
- ☐ Test/personal/portfolio (not for commercial use)
- ☐ Other ______________________________ *(specify)*
- ☐ Brochure
- ☐ Point of Sale
- ☐ Inserts
- ☐ Poster ______________________________ *(specify)*
- ☐ Packaging
- ☐ Television/Cinema/Video
- ☐ Full library use

Territory

- ☐ UK
- ☐ Single EC country ____________________ *(specify)*
- ☐ Continental Europe
- ☐ USA
- ☐ English language areas (book publishing)
- ☐ Worldwide
- ☐ Other ______________________________ *(specify)*

Period of Use

- ☐ One year
- ☐ Two years
- ☐ Other ______________________________ *(specify)*

For specific restrictions/conditions/agreements see attached.
Electronic rights must be negotiated separately.

*I/We understand that the image shall be deemed to represent an imaginary person unless agreed otherwise, in writing, by my agent or myself.

*I/We understand that I/we have no interest in the copyright, nor any moral rights, in the photograph.

**I am over 18 years of age.

Name of *model/model agency : *(print)* ______________________________

Signature of *model/model agency : ______________________________ Date : ____________________

***Parent/guardian or model agency must sign for models under 18 years of age.*

In accepting the above release it is the responsibility of the *photographer/agency/client not to use or authorise the use of the material except for the above media, territories and time periods. Further usage must be negotiated and agreed beforehand, in writing, with the *model/model agency.

**Delete as appropriate*

ISSUED IN 1995 BY THE ASSOCIATION OF PHOTOGRAPHERS LTD, THE ASSOCIATION OF MODEL AGENTS AND THE INSTITUTE OF PRACTITIONERS IN ADVERTISING

ILLUSTRATION 6

Suggested Guidelines for Negotiating Further Usage Fees for Advertising Photography

Introduction

These guidelines are for use where the photographer has issued, or is issuing, a licence and were produced as a result of discussions between art buyers, photographers and photographers' agents. These are not recommendations, but are provided as guidelines for negotiation based on current trade practice.

In the UK, the photographer's fee normally includes the first use of the photograph/s, but the fee may differ according to duration of the licence, media use and territory, as well as factors such as the experience of the photographer and the desirability of the commission.

Base Usage Rate

To prevent misunderstandings when negotiating additional usage fees, it has been suggested that a Base Usage Rate (BUR) should be established. The BUR should be clearly stated on the photographer's original estimate and should not be less than the negotiated day rate.

When the photographer's involvement is greater than a single day rate would suggest, a higher BUR could be agreed.

When several images from a single day's shoot ie. the same subject or variations from a single shoot, are used by the commissioner, then each individual image should be subject to a negotiable BUR, at less than the original commissioned day rate agreed.

Exclusivity

Clients and advertising agencies are concerned that the photographs which they commission, and for which they pay the origination expenses, should not fall into the hands of competitors or become associated with other products after the initial licence period has finished.

To prevent this, it has been suggested that the photographer should not sell the photographs, for example through a library, without client and agency permission, for four years after the end of the licence (unless otherwise agreed). This should be negotiated with the individual agency/client before the shoot takes place, as should other related issues such as confidentiality. Where material is not sensitive, it is unlikely that an agency or their client would withhold this permission.

On expiry of the initial exclusivity period, the commissioner should be offered first option to extend the exclusivity clause at a negotiated rate.

First Use **(UK or any single EU country)**

1 Year

Any two of the following media:

Press	TV
Poster	*Brochure
Point of Sale	*Packaging
Direct Mail	Merchandising ('purchasable' or 'give away')

(3rd media may be included depending on its proportion of the media spend)

2 Years

Any one of the above media

Additional Media during 1 or 2 year licence

Press	100% BUR
Poster	100% BUR
Point of Sale	25-50% BUR
Direct Mail	25-50% BUR
TV	25-50% BUR
Internet	**10-25% BUR + credit where possible
CD	10% BUR + credit where possible

Extended licence period:

1st year extension

Press	100% BUR
Poster	100% BUR
Point of Sale	25-50% BUR
Direct Mail	25-50% BUR
TV	25-50% BUR
Internet	**10-25% BUR + credit where possible
CD	10% BUR + credit where possible

2nd year and subsequent year's extension

Press	50% BUR
Poster	50% BUR
Point of Sale	12.5-25% BUR
Direct Mail	12.5-25% BUR
TV	12.5-25% BUR
Internet	negotiable
CD	negotiable

Other Media

Other media should be negotiated separately, eg. video, T-Shirts ('purchasable' or 'give away'). Negotiations could be based on one of the above media which commands the same public interest, eg. viewing figures. Negotiations for purchasable items could be based on a percentage of the guaranteed projection, plus a royalty.

First Use outside EU

Where photographs are commissioned initially for use outside the European Union, the negotiating base is usually for a single media, for a period of 1 year only.

Secondary Usage

Different geographical areas (refer to Additional Territories Usage Chart)
For all secondary and subsequent use of photographs, it has been agreed that the percentages given on the attached tables are reasonable and fair. However, it is impossible to cover every eventuality and it is for the photographer and/or their agent and the agency or client to negotiate an arrangement which both parties find agreeable.

All Uses Licence

In principle, we are opposed to the assignment of copyright. However, we recognise that agencies sometimes need to negotiate a fee covering any future use of the photographs without continuous reference to the photographer.

In such cases, the Licence to Use will specify "All Media" under Media Use, the Territory will be "Worldwide" and the Time Period will be "Unlimited".

The licence will be exclusive to the Agency/Client and will cover all uses of the photography in relation to the product named on the licence. The photographer retains the right to use the photographs for promoting his/her own work.

The All Uses licence is subject to the general Terms and Conditions and therefore does not permit use in relation to another product or sub-licensing, for example to a photolibrary.

* *These media should have separate negotiations when requested as an additional media; dependent on print runs and 'life span'.*

** *% is dependant on context. Credit to be given on lead page where possible.*

SUGGESTED GUIDELINES FOR NEGOTIATING USAGE FEES FOR ADDITIONAL TERRITORIES

Territory	Principle Media	Single Additional Media	Multi Media*	2nd Year	3rd Year
Europe (not in EU)	100%	50-100%	150%	100% of 1st Year	50% of 1st Year
Middle East	100%	50-100%	150%	100% of 1st Year	50% of 1st Year
Single Additional Country	20-50%	10-25%	75%	100% of 1st Year	50% of 1st Year
European Union	200%	50-100%	300%	100% of 1st Year	50% of 1st Year
USA	200%	50-100%	300%	100% of 1st Year	50% of 1st Year
South America	100%	25-50%	150%	100% of 1st Year	50% of 1st Year
Canada	50%	12.5-25%	75%	100% of 1st Year	50% of 1st Year
Africa	100%	25-50%	150%	100% of 1st Year	50% of 1st Year
Asia (excluding Japan)	75%	20-35%	110%	100% of 1st Year	50% of 1st Year
Asia (including Japan)	175%	50-75%	250%	100% of 1st Year	50% of 1st Year
Japan	100%	25-50%	150%	100% of 1st Year	50% of 1st Year
Oceana/Australasia	100%	25-50%	150%	100% of 1st Year	50% of 1st Year
Worldwide	500%	125-250%	750%	100% of 1st Year	50% of 1st Year
International Media **	100-200%	N/A	N/A	100% of 1st Year	50% of 1st Year
All Uses Licence	In excess of 750%				

Please Note: All percentages are of the Base Usage Rate (BUR).
Where the single additional exposure is very small, the lower percentage should be negotiated.
See overleaf for Territory breakdown by country.

* *Any combination (three plus) of the media listed on the previous pages.*
** *In flight magazines, Time, Newsweek, National Geographic, etc.*

ILLUSTRATION 7

Australasia/Oceana

Australia
Tasmania
New Zealand
Fiji
Israel
Jordan
Oman
Syria
Saudi Arabia
United Arab Emirates

Asia

Afghanistan
Bangladesh
China
India
Indonesia
Indochina
Japan
Korea
Malaysia
Mongolia
Myanmar (formerly Burma)
Pakistan
Philippines
Sri Lanka
Syria
Taiwan
Thailand
Vietnam

European Union

Austria
Belgium
Denmark
Finland
France
Germany
Greece
Irish Republic
Italy
Luxembourg
Netherlands
Portugal
Spain
Sweden
UK

Europe - not EU

Albania
Armenia*
Azerbaijan*
Belarus*
Bosnia-Herzegovina
Bulgaria
Croatia
Cyprus
Czech Republic
Estonia
Faroe Islands
Georgia*
Greenland
Hungary
Iceland
Kazakhstan*
Kirghizstan*
Latvia
Liechenstein
Lithuania
Macedonia
Malta
Moldova*
Montenegro
Norway
Poland
Romania
Russia*
Serbia
Slovak Republic
Slovenia
Spitzbergen
Switzerland
Tajikistan*
Turkey
Turkmenistan*
Ukraine*
Uzbekistan*

**former USSR*

Middle East

Egypt
Iran
Iraq
Samoa
Tonga
Papua New Guinea
Pacific Islands

South America

Argentina
Bolivia
Brazil
Chile
Colombia
Ecuador
Paraguay
Peru
Uruguay
Venezuela

Agent/Photographer Agreement

Agreement dated .... between .... (hereafter called The Agent)

and .... (hereafter called The Photographer).

Territory

The Agent will represent The Photographer in the following geographical areas: ....

Field of Photographer

The Agent will represent The Photographer in the following fields of work: ....

Responsibilities

The Agent will:

a) solicit photographic assignments on behalf of The Photographer;
b) negotiate contracts and fees with the client as agreed with The Photographer;

The Photographer will:

a) provide a portfolio of work to a standard agreed by both parties;
b) update and replace work in the folio as necessary.

Responsibility for collection, storage and mounting of published work/tear sheets for the portfolio, shall be with the Agent/Photographer*.

Accounting

- The Agent/Photographer* is responsible for estimates, VAT invoices, and licences on Agent/Photographer* letterhead.
- VAT invoice to client to be raised by The Agent/Photographer*, promptly on completion and acceptance of the commission.
- Payment to The Photographer, less commission, to be made 5 days after receipt and clearance of the client's cheque/Commission payment to Agent to be made ....*
- Statements of account to be sent on a monthly basis and outstanding debts chased by The Agent/Photographer* on a regular basis.
- The Agent/Photographer* will keep an accurate and up to date book of accounts which can be checked on demand by The Agent/Photographer.
- Copies of orders, estimates, invoices and licenses to be kept by both parties.
- VAT returns, accountant and auditing fees are the responsibility of the Agent/Photographer*.

House Accounts

The following are live client accounts held by The Photographer at the date of this agreement, on which no commission is due to The Agent unless otherwise agreed as, and when, future commissions are negotiated:

....	....	....
....	....	....
....	....	....
....	....	....

Commission Structure/Calculation

- Commission is payable to The Agent at ....% of The Photographer's fee (excluding expenses) on jobs solicited and confirmed by The Agent.

- Commission is payable to The Agent at ....% of The Photographer's fee (excluding expenses) on jobs solicited and confirmed by The Photographer, but not on the above House Accounts.
- The fee shall be deemed to be the balance of the invoice (excluding VAT) after actual expenses are deducted.
- Commission is payable to The Agent at ....% on re-usage fees of work originally solicited and confirmed by The Agent.
- The Photographer reserves the right to refuse work solicited by The Agent.
- Commission shall not be payable if for whatever reason any work is not completed.

Promotional/Portfolio Costs

- Promotional material and advertising costs will be borne by: ....
- Content of promotional and advertising material shall be to a standard agreed by both parties.

Expenses

Travel, telephone, office administration, entertainment, delivery and general business expenses incurred by The Agent will be paid by The Agent.

Insurance

The Agent/Photographer* confirms that, as of the date of this agreement, insurance to cover the portfolio and its contents to the sum of £............. is now in effect and will be maintained throughout the term of this agreement.

Termination

This agreement shall terminate 30 days after receipt of written notice of termination given by either party, subject to the following provisions:

On termination of this agreement by either The Agent or The Photographer:

a) The Agent will receive commission of ....% on work in progress or previously arranged.

b) The Agent will receive commission of ....% for a period of .... months from the date of termination on work received by The Photographer from clients previously solicited on his/her behalf by The Agent.

c) The Agent will for a period of .... months from the date of termination, pass on all enquiries from past or future clients to The Photographer or the new agent.

- Throughout the term of this agreement, the portfolio remains the property of The Photographer and will be returned into his/her possession immediately on termination.
- The relationship between The Photographer and The Agent shall be that of principal and agent, and nothing contained herein shall constitute this arrangement a joint venture or partnership. The Agent shall not acquire any rights in any of The Photographer's work.
- This agreement constitutes the entire understanding between the parties and no modifications shall be of any force and effect unless made in writing and signed by both parties.
- This agreement is governed by the laws of England and Wales, to the non-exclusive jurisdiction of whose courts the parties submit.

Signed

.... On behalf of The Agent

.... On behalf of The Photographer

** delete as appropriate*

THE ASSOCIATION OF PHOTOGRAPHERS 1993

PHOTOGRAPHERS CONTRACT

AN AGREEMENT

made this . . . . day of . . . . 19 . . .

BETWEEN . . . .

of . . . .

. . . .

HEREINAFTER CALLED the 'Photographer' which expression shall, where the context admits, include the Photographer's executors, administrators and assigns. [NB for collections of illustrations the 'Photographer'shall be altered to the 'Proprietor']

AND . . . .

. . . .

HEREINAFTER CALLED the 'Agent' which expression shall, where the context admits, include the Agent's executors, administrators and assigns or successors in business.

WHEREBY it is mutually agreed between the parties hereto as follows:

The material 1] The Photographer has created original photographs in b/w and colour consisting of approximately [ ] exposures as set out in schedule A attached hereto and hereinafter referred to as the 'material'.

Delivery and Property 2] The Photographer undertakes to deliver the material, correctly and properly captioned, on the signing by both parties of this Agreement. The property in the material shall remain with the Photographer who shall at his discretion insure the replacement value thereof. While proper care will be taken of the material the Agent shall not be responsible for any loss or damage to the material however caused.

Warranty 3] The Photographer hereby warrants to the Agent that the material is his original work, that he has not entered into any agreement in respect of the material which would adversely affect the rights granted other than arrangements and restrictions specifically noted to the Agent, that he owns the copyright of the material, that he holds appropriate consents from copyright owners, in respect of photographs reproducing other copyright material, eg. paintings, that a model release is available unless stated to the contrary and that he has the full power to make this agreement and will indemnify the Agent against any loss, damage or expense occasioned to the Agent in consequence of any breach of this warranty.

3a] The Agency hereby warrants that it is a member of BAPLA, subscribing to it's Code of Conduct for Members and will use every endevour to sell the material at the best obtainable prices.

4] The Photographer undertakes not to assign, license or otherwise dispose of the copyright in the material and undertakes not to license, assign or dispose of any interest in other photographs which for any reason may cause confusion or which may derogate from the rights granted by this Agreement, without permission of the Agency. This undertaking is limited to the term of the Agreement.

Rights and Assignment *[delete whichever is inapplicable]* 5] In consideration of the payments hereinafter mentioned the Photographer hereby grants to the Agency the exclusive right to license the reproduction of the material for the term of this Agreement *throughout the world/in the territories listed below.*

Payments *[delete whichever is inapplicable]* 6] The Agency's rate of commission shall be . . . .* per centum [. . . .%] of all monies received by the Agency as revenues including compensation for loss, earned by the material placed with the Agency by the Photographer. The Agency will settle with the Photographer *quarterly/monthly* in respect of all relevant paid-up accounts.

Audit	7]	The Photographer shall have the right, upon written request, to appoint an auditor to examine the account books of the Agent insofar as they relate to the sales of his own material. This audit will be at his own expense. Should an error in excess of 10% of sums due be discovered as a consequence of such an audit, the Agency will pay the fees.
Competing work and Option *delete a or b if inapplicable*	8a]	During the continuance of this Agreement the Photographer will give the agent a first option on any other photographs in which he holds the copyright [other than commissioned photographs or photographs for the personal use of the Photographer].
	8b]	Any photographs given by the Photographer to the Agent will be on the same terms as this Agreement subject always to the provisions of Clauses 3 and 4 above unless agreed otherwise in writing.
Term	9]	Any photographs deposited with the Agency by the Photographer will be retained by the Agency for a minimum period of 36 months from the date of their deposit. Thereafter either party may give 12 months written notice of termination. Termination shall not prejudice licensing agreements then extant and all negotiations which the Agent has properly entered into with any third party. On the date of termination no further licenses shall be granted. The material shall be returned to the Photographer as soon as possible after termination and in any case all reasonable endevours will be made to return the material within 12 months.
Agreement	10]	This Agreement constitutes the entire undertaking of the parties hereto and may not be amended, changed, altered, varied or otherwise modified except by an instrument in writing signed by both parties.
Arbitration	11]	If any dispute shall arise between the Photographer and the Agent out of or in connection with or in relation to this Agreement, the matter should be left to be resolved by the courts.
Law	12]	This Agreement shall be governed by and interpreted in all respects in accordance with the Law of England.

AS WITNESS THE HANDS OF THE PARTIES

Schedule A

.... [For the Agent]

.... [For the Photographer]

ILLUSTRATION 9

2/94

When detaching a page, please leave this stub intact on the remaining pages.

Inland Revenue

Details of employee leaving work — Copy for Tax Office

P45 Part 1

1 PAYE Reference — District number / Reference number

2 Employee's National Insurance number

3 Surname (in capitals) — (Mr Mrs Miss Ms)

First name(s) (in capitals)

4 Leaving date (in figures) — Day / Month / Year 19

5 Tax Code at leaving date. *If Week 1 or Month 1 basis applies, write 'X' in the box marked* Week 1 or Month 1 — Code / Week 1 or Month 1

6 Last entries on *Deductions Working Sheet* (P11) ***Complete only if Tax Code is cumulative.*** *Make no entry here if Week 1 or Month 1 basis applies. Go to item 7.*

- Week or month number — Week / Month
- Total pay to date £ p
- Total tax to date £ p

7 This employment pay and tax. *No entry needed if Tax Code is cumulative and amounts are same as item 6 entry.*

- Total pay in this employment £ p
- Total tax in this employment £ p

8 Works number/ Payroll number

9 Department or branch if any

10 Employee's private address and Postcode

11 I certify that the details entered above in items 1 to 9 are correct

Employer's name, address and Postcode

Date

To the employer

- Complete this form following the 'Employee leaving' instructions in the *Employer's Basic Guide to PAYE* (P8). Make sure the details are clear on all four parts of this form. Make sure your name and address is shown on Parts 1 and 1A.
- Detach Part 1 and send it to your Tax Office immediately.
- Hand Parts 1A, 2 and 3 (unseparated) to your employee when he or she leaves.
- If the employee has died, write 'D' in this box and send all four parts of this form (unseparated) to your Tax Office immediately.

For Tax Office use

P45(1996)

CCO 10/95

ILLUSTRATION 10

Inland Revenue

HM Customs & Excise

CONTRIBUTIONS AGENCY

An Executive Agency of the Department of Social Security

For official use only

Use this form to tell the Contributions Agency, the Inland Revenue, and Customs and Excise that you have started self-employment. It is not a registration form for Value Added Tax (VAT) but if you need more information about any of the following please put a 'X' in the relevant box.

VAT ☐ Customs ☐ Excise ☐

Send the completed form to **Contributions Agency Class 2 Group Longbenton Newcastle upon Tyne NE98 1YX.**

The Contributions Agency will send a copy of the completed form to the Inland Revenue, and if you put 'X' in one of the boxes aside, Customs and Excise.

Notification of Self Employment

Yourself

Your surname

Your title, *for example, Mr/Mrs/ Miss/ Ms*

Your first name(s)

Your date of birth *(in figures)* Day ☐ Month ☐ Year 19

Your home address

Postcode

Your home phone number (include *STD code)*

Your National Insurance number: Letters ☐ Numbers ☐ Numbers ☐ Numbers ☐ Letter ☐

Your marital status – *put 'X' in relevant box*

Single ☐ Married ☐ Widowed ☐

Separated ☐ Divorced ☐

Tax Office to which you sent your last Tax Return

Reference in that Tax Office

Your business

1 When did you start in business or when will you start? Day ☐ Month ☐ Year 19

2 What sort of self employed work do you do / will you do?

If you are working in the fishing industry as a Sharefisherman put 'X' in this box ☐

Your business continued

3 What is your business name and address?

Postcode

Your business phone number *(include STD code)*

Your business fax number *(include STD code)*

4 What is your position in the business? *For example, owner, partner. If you are a subcontractor, put 'subcontractor'.*

5 Do you have any business partners? *Put 'X' in the relevant box* No ☐ Yes ☐

If you have answered 'No', please go to question 6.

If you have answered 'Yes', please state

Partner's surname

Partner's first name(s)

Partner's address

Postcode

If you have more than one partner, please give details on a separate sheet.

6 How do you wish to pay your Class 2 National Insurance contributions? *Put 'X' in the relevant box*

- by quarterly bill ☐
- by Direct Debit – *complete the attached application form CA5601 and send it with this form.* ☐

Do you want more information about exception from liability because of low earnings or deferment? *If so, put 'X' in the relevant box*

- exception from liability because of low earnings ☐
- deferment (if you are both employed and self employed) ☐

CWF 1 *(formerly 41G/CF11)* CC01/96

Please turn over

ILLUSTRATION 11

Your business continued

7 Do you employ anybody, including members of your family, to work in your business?

Put 'X' in the relevant box No ☐ Yes ☐

If you have answered 'No', please go to question 8.
If you have answered 'Yes', read the statements below and put 'X' in the boxes that apply to your employees.

I have employees who earn

- £61 a week or £265 a month or more but less than £72.50 a week or £314 a month ☐
- £72.50 a week or £314 a month or more ☐
- more than £1 a week and have other employment ☐

8 If you took over an existing business, what was the name and address of the person you acquired it from?

Postcode

9 If you are, or will be, doing all your work for one person or firm, state their name and address

Postcode

Your previous employment

10 What were you doing before you started this self employment? If you were unemployed, please state what you were doing **before** you became unemployed. ***Put 'X' in the relevant box below.***

I was employed – ***give your employer's name and address below, the date the employment ended, and go to 11.*** ☐

I was self employed – ***give your business name and address below, the date the business ceased trading and go to 12.*** ☐

I was in full time education – ***give the date the education finished and go to 13.*** ☐

Name and address of employer/business

Postcode

	Day	Month	Year
Date employment/ business/education ended			19

Previous employment continued

11 If you were employed and you have a leaving certificate form P45 from your last employer

- keep Part 1A
- attach Parts 2 and 3 to this form and put 'X' in this box to show that you have done so. ☐

Tax Returns

To make sure that the Inland Revenue sends you a Tax Return suited to your needs under Self Assessment, please answer these questions.

12 Do you have, in addition to the self employment described on this form, any other paid employment or an existing business which you will continue to run?

Put 'X' in the relevant box No ☐ Yes ☐

If you have answered 'No', please go to question 13.
If you have answered 'Yes', please put 'X' in the box(es) that apply to you.

- I am in paid employment as well as being self employed ☐
- I have an existing business as well as this self employment ☐

Name and address of employer/existing business

Postcode

13 Do you have an agent to advise you on your tax affairs?

Put 'X' in the relevant box No ☐ Yes ☐

If you have answered 'No', please go to the Declaration below.
If you have answered 'Yes', please state

Agent's name and address

Postcode

Agent's phone number ***(include STD code)***

Declaration

This is my notification of self employment and I have given details of my business on this form.

I understand and agree that the information on this form will be made available to the Contributions Agency, Inland Revenue and Customs and Excise.

Signed

	Day	Month	Year
Date ***(in figures)***			19

ILLUSTRATION 11

CA 72B (CF 359) (1996/97) Contributions Agency, Department of Social Security.

Application for deferment of payment of Class 2 and Class 4 contributions for the year 6 April 1996 to 5 April 1997

Please read this leaflet and then fill in the application form and send it to the Contributions Agency, Deferment Group, Longbenton, Newcastle upon Tyne, NE98 1YX.

If you are not sure if you will qualify for deferment or have any queries regarding the completion of this form, you can call the Deferment Group Helpline on 06451 57141. Calls will be charged at BT local rates.

If this is your first notification of self-employment, send the completed application form together with form CF 11 to Contributions Agency, Class 2 Group, Longbenton, Newcastle upon Tyne, NE98 1YX.

1 Surname (BLOCK CAPITALS)

2 Other names (BLOCK CAPITALS)

3 Mr/Mrs/Miss/Ms or Title

4 National Insurance number

5 Date of birth

/ /

6 Address (If you change your address you must advise Deferment Group)

Postcode

7 Telephone number including std code

8 If you want correspondence on this subject to be sent direct to an accountant or adviser please give the address below

Postcode

9 Telephone number including std code

10 If you are a married woman/widow, do you hold a valid certificate of election?

Yes No

Earnings as an employee

11a Enter all earnings (actual or estimated) as an employee. If your earnings are more than £24,115 you need only insert £24,115 (Class 1 contributions will normally be paid on such income).

£

11b Please give the nature of your employment

11c Are any of these earnings chargeable to income tax under case I or II of Schedule D?

Yes No

Important: please read and sign the declaration overleaf

ILLUSTRATION 12

Self-employed earnings – these are separate to earnings as an employee quoted above

12a Enter all earnings (actual or estimated) from self-employment (Class 2 contributions will normally be paid on such income). If your earnings are more than £23,660 you need only insert £23,660. Self-employed earnings below £3,430 will be considered for exception.

£

12b Name of your tax district

12c Please give your Schedule D tax reference number

12d Please give the nature of your self-employment

12e Please state date self-employment started

/ /

Declaration

I apply for deferment of payment of Class 4 (and if appropriate Class 2) contributions as determined by the Contributions Agency under the Social Security Contributions and Benefits Act 1992 for the 1996/97 year only.

I understand that if a shortfall of contributions arises a request for further payment will be made and I will provide the information necessary to calculate any outstanding contributions.

I undertake to pay arrears within 28 days of demand. I accept that consideration will not be given to further deferment applications if a liability remains outstanding.

Signature

Date

/ /

Official use

Tick box

- CF 11 enclosed detached
- Quarterly bill account opened
- Quarterly bill account inhibited

An Executive Agency of the Department of Social Security

CF 10 (1996/97) Contributions Agency, Department of Social Security.

Application for exception from liability for Class 2 contributions

You should read the attached leaflet before filling in this form. Ask at the Social Security office if you need more information.

If you are newly self-employed you will need to complete form CF 11 (Notification of self-employment), if you have not already done so.

1 Surname (BLOCK CAPITALS)

2 Other names (BLOCK CAPITALS)

3 Mr/Mrs/Miss/Ms or Title

4 National Insurance number

5 Date of birth

/ /

6 When did your present self-employment begin?

/ /

7 Full address

Postcode Telephone

8 Business address (if different from above)

Postcode Telephone

9 What is your occupation when self-employed? If you have more than one occupation please give details on a separate sheet.

10 What are your expected net earnings from self-employment for the year beginning 6 April 1996? (See page 9 of this leaflet).

£

Complete either section A or B and complete the declaration

Section A: Complete this section if your self-employment is more than a spare-time activity, or is your only source of income.

Part 1: Complete in all cases.
Do you want to pay contributions voluntarily?

☐ Yes (See page 13) ☐ No

Part 2: Complete if you have been self-employed for less than 12 months.
Have you read the section headed 'Newly self-employed' on page 7 of this leaflet?

☐ Yes ☐ No

Please complete the declaration overleaf.

Part 3: Complete if you have been self-employed for more than 12 months. The information you give will be treated as confidential. What is the last tax or accounting year for which you have earnings figures? (Enter dates)

From / / To / /

In that period what were your total earnings after deductions?

£

(See page 9)

Note: To support your application you must send in with this form your accounts for the last accounting period, some evidence of earnings, or tax papers which have been agreed with the Inland Revenue, (see page 8 of this leaflet). If the accounts are with your accountant or some other person and you agree to our asking him or her to produce them, give us his or her name and address opposite. Nil tax assessements are not accepted as evidence of earnings.

Name and address of person accounts are with

Postcode Telephone

Now please complete the declaration on the back of this form

ILLUSTRATION 13

Section B: Complete this section if you have earnings from spare-time self-employment.

If you work for one or more employers for livelihood and your self-employment is only a spare-time activity, please give estimates for the year beginning 6 April 1996.

Earnings from employment*	Name of employer
£	

Earnings from employment*	Name of employer
£	

*If more than £23,660 put 'over £23,660'. (If you have more than two employers please give details on a separate sheet of paper.)

Now complete the declaration below

Declaration

I have read this leaflet and declare that the information given on this form is true and complete to the best of my knowledge and belief.

I enclose:	Yes	No
▶ last years accounts		
▶ my Certificate of small earnings exception		
▶ my income tax papers		
▶ my completed CF 11 I am newly self-employed.		

Tear off the form and send it to the Contributions Agency, Class 2 Group, Department of Social Security, Longbenton, Newcastle upon Tyne, NE98 1YX

Please keep this leaflet for reference

Signature

Date / /

For official use

	From	To	AO INTLS	Date	EO INTLS
Application received. Management inhibition set					
Self-employment disregarded DL/CC(N)12 issued					
QB account amended/deleted as appropriate					
See allowed					
QB account noted					
CF 17/CA 08 issued					
CF 400 issued to NIRS of SEE award					
Management inhibition unset					
Application rejected DL/CC(N)13 issued					
Management inhibition unset					
See cancelled Confirmed QB account open					

An Executive Agency of the Department of Social Security

ILLUSTRATION 13

HM Customs
and Excise

Value Added Tax

Application for Registration

For office use	Issuing office
Issue code: ______ - ______ Date of receipt: ______	

ILLUSTRATION 14

VAT 1 Page 1 PCU(November 1995)

Value Added Tax

Application for Registration

Before you start, please read the Notice "Should I be registered for VAT?". The notes in part 2 will help you to answer the questions on this form. If you do not answer the questions correctly it may take longer to register you and give you a registration number. Write clearly in black ink and use CAPITAL LETTERS.

1 Please give your full name
- *if you are a limited company give your company name*
- *if you are a partnership give your trading name. If you do not have a trading name give the names of all the partners*

Name:

2 Please give your trading name (if different from the name given at 1)

Trading name:

3 Please give the address of your principal place of business
- *this should be where the day-to-day running of your business takes place*

Business address:

Postcode:

Phone no:

Fax no:

4 Describe your main business activity

5 Who owns the business?
- *If you are a partnership please remember to fill in form VAT 2 as well as this form*

Please tick ☑

Limited company ☐ Give details from your certificate of incorporation:

Certificate number | Date of certificate

Sole proprietor ☐ Partnership ☐

Other ☐ If other, give details below:

6 (a) Has your business been transferred to you as a going concern?
- *only give details here if you are taking over an existing business from someone else or if you have changed the legal status of your business*

Please tick ☑

Yes ☐ Give details below: No ☐ Go to 7

Date of transfer

Name of previous owner

VAT registration number of previous owner

VAT 1 Page 1R (11/95)

ILLUSTRATION 14

6 (b) Do you want to keep the previous owner's VAT number?

- *to keep the number you and the previous owner will have to fill in a form VAT 68 as well*

Please tick ☑

Yes ☐ No ☐

7 Please give your bank details

- *this question must be completed in all cases*

Bank sort code ☐☐☐☐☐☐ Account number ☐☐☐☐☐☐☐☐

or Girobank account number ☐☐☐☐☐☐☐☐☐

Please tick box if you do not have a bank account: ☐

8 Do you use a computer for accounting?

- *if you use a computer let us know the type of computer and software you use, in a separate letter*

Please tick ☑

Yes ☐ No ☐

9 Have you made any taxable supplies yet?

- *if you are not sure what '**taxable supply**' means paragraph 2 in part 1 of the Notice will help you*
- *if you have not yet made any taxable supplies **you must enclose evidence** to show that you are going to in the future*

Please tick ☑

Yes ☐ I made my first supply on

No ☐ but I intend to start on

10 Have your taxable supplies in the past 12 months or less gone over the registration limit?

Please tick ☑

Yes ☐ I went over the limit on

No ☐

11 Do you expect the taxable supplies you will make in the next 30 days alone will go over the registration limit?

Please tick ☑

Yes ☐ Go to 12

No ☐ Go to 13

12 From what date must you be registered for VAT?

- *if you have answered Yes to either question 10 or 11 then give the date from which you **have** to be registered (note 12 in part 2 of the Notice will help you)*
- *if you want to be registered from an earlier date fill in the date in the box provided*

I have to be registered from

I would like to be registered from this earlier date

13 I do not need to be registered but I want to be registered

- *only answer this question if you have not yet reached the registration limit but want to be registered on a voluntary basis*

I want to be registered from

14 Please give the value of taxable supplies you think you will make in the next 12 months

- *remember to include zero-rated supplies in this figure*

ILLUSTRATION 14

VAT 1 Page 2(11/95)

15 What value of goods are you likely to sell to or buy from other European Union countries in the next 12 months?

Sell £ ______

Buy £ ______

16 Do you want exemption from registration because all your supplies are zero-rated?

- *if you are asking for exemption from registration enter the expected value of your zero-rated supplies in the next 12 months, in the box provided.*

Please tick ☑

Yes ☐

No ☐

Value of zero-rated supplies £ ______

17 Do you think you will be repaid VAT regularly?

- *tick Yes if you think the VAT on what you sell will normally be less than the VAT on what you buy*

Please tick ☑

Yes ☐ No ☐

18 Are there any other VAT registrations you are, or have been involved in, in the last 24 months?

- *give the registration numbers of any businesses you have been involved in, in the boxes provided. If you are a partnership or a limited company this means any businesses which any partners or directors have been involved in*
- *Continue on a separate sheet if necessary*

Please tick ☑

Yes ☐ No ☐

Registration numbers of other businesses:

19 Please complete and sign the declaration

Declaration

I, ______

(enter your full name in CAPITAL LETTERS) declare that the information given on this form and contained in any accompanying document is true and complete.

Signature ______

Mr, Mrs, Miss, Ms

Date ______

Please tick ☑

Proprietor ☐ Director ☐

Trustee ☐ Partner ☐

Company Secretary ☐ Authorised official ☐

For office use

Local office code and registration number ______

EDR D M Y

Stagger ☐ Status ☐

Name ______

Trade name ______

Trade classification ______

Taxable Turnover ______

Rept. ☐ Vol. ☐ Oversize name address ☐ Comp. user ☐ Group Div ☐ Intg ☐ Overseas ☐ Intg. EC ☐

Value of Sales to EC ______

Value of Purchases from EC ______

VAT 1 Page 2R(11/95)

ILLUSTRATION 14

HM Customs and Excise

Value Added Tax Return

For the period

to

For Official Use

Registration number | Period

You could be liable to a financial penalty if your completed return and all the VAT payable are not received by the due date.

Due date:

For official use D O R only	

Fold | Here

Before you fill in this form please read the notes on the back and the VAT leaflet *"Filling in your VAT return"*. Fill in all boxes clearly in ink, and write 'none' where necessary. Don't put a dash or leave any box blank. If there are no pence write **"00"** in the pence column. **Do not** enter more than one amount in any box.

For official use

		£	p
VAT due in this period on **sales** and other outputs	1		
VAT due in this period on **acquisitions** from other **EC Member States**	2		
Total VAT due **(the sum of boxes 1 and 2)**	3		
VAT reclaimed in this period on **purchases** and other inputs (including acquisitions from the EC)	4		
Net VAT to be paid to Customs or reclaimed by you **(Difference between boxes 3 and 4)**	5		
Total value of **sales** and all other outputs excluding any VAT. **Include your box 8 figure**	6		00
Total value of **purchases** and all other inputs excluding any VAT. **Include your box 9 figure**	7		00
Total value of all **supplies** of goods and related services, excluding any VAT, to other **EC Member States**	8		00
Total value of all **acquisitions** of goods and related services, excluding any VAT, from other **EC Member States**	9		00

Retail schemes. If you have used any of the schemes in the period covered by this return, enter the relevant letter(s) in this box.

If you are enclosing a payment please tick this box.

DECLARATION: You, or someone on your behalf, must sign below.

I, ...declare that the
(Full name of signatory in BLOCK LETTERS)

information given above is true and complete.

Signature ....Date ....19.............

A false declaration can result in prosecution.

VAT 100 (Full)

PCU (June 1996)

ILLUSTRATION 15

Notes

These notes and the VAT leaflet *Filling in your VAT Return* will help you fill in this form. You may also need to refer to other VAT notices and leaflets.

If you need help or advice please contact your local VAT office.

If you are using the 'cash accounting scheme', the amounts of VAT due and deductible are for payments you actually receive and make, and not on invoices you receive and send out.

If you put **minus figures** in boxes 1 to 3, or are entering a sum **DUE** to Customs in box 4, please enclose the figure in brackets.

Amounts not declared correctly on previous return

1. If any of your previous returns declared too much or too little VAT that has not yet been accounted for, you can correct the position using boxes 1 and 4 for net amounts of **£2000 or less.**

2. If the net amount is **over £2000**, tell your local VAT office immediately. Don't include the amount on this return.

If you do not follow these instructions you could be liable to a financial penalty.

How to pay your VAT

Cross all cheques and postal orders "AC Payee Only" make them payable to "H M Customs and Excise" and put a line through any spaces on the "pay" line.

In your own interest do not send notes, coins, or uncrossed postal orders by post.

If you wish to pay by 'credit transfer', ask your local VAT office. Pre-printed booklets of credit transfer slips will be sent to you.

Please write your VAT registration number on the back of all cheques and bank giro credit slips.

Where to send this return

You must make sure your completed form and any VAT payable are received by the 'due date' (shown over the page) by:

The Controller
VAT Central Unit
H M Customs and Excise
21 Victoria Avenue
Southend-on-Sea X
SS99 1AA.

Complaints

The Adjudicator reviews complaints not settled to your satisfaction by Customs. The recommendations of the Adjudicator are independent and the service is free. It covers complaints not general enquiries. [Telephone the Adjudicator on 0171 930 2292].

VAT 100 (Full) Reverse (06/96)

Box 1

Show the VAT due on all goods and services you supplied in this period.

Box 2

Show the VAT due (but not paid) on all goods and related services you acquired in this period from other EC Member States.

Box 3

Show the total amount of the VAT due ie the sum of boxes 1 and 2. This is your total **Output** tax.

Box 4

Show the amount of VAT deductible on any business purchases including acquisitions of goods and related services from other EC Member States. This is your **Input** tax.

Box 5

If this amount is under £1, you need not send any payment, nor will any repayment be made to you, but you must still fill in this form and send it to the VAT Central Unit.

Boxes 6 and 7

In box 6 show the value excluding VAT of your total outputs (supplies of goods and services). Include zero rated, exempt outputs and EC supplies from box 8.

In box 7 show the value excluding VAT of all your inputs (purchases of goods and services). Include zero rated, exempt inputs and EC acquisitions from box 9.

Boxes 8 and 9

EC TRADE ONLY

Use these boxes if you have supplied goods to or acquired goods from another EC Member State. Include related services such as transport costs where these form part of the invoice or contract price. The figures should exclude VAT.

The other EC Member States are: Belgium, Denmark, France, Germany, Greece, Netherlands, Ireland, Italy, Luxembourg, Portugal, Spain, Austria, Finland and Sweden.

You must tell your local VAT office about any changes in your business circumstances (including changes of address).

Cash Book : BANK RECEIPTS - A. Photographer - Period 1/04/95 - 31/03/96

Date	Detail	Invoice No	Gross	Sales NET	Sales VAT	Sundries
	Totals					

ILLUSTRATION 16

Photographers Cash Book : BANK PAYMENTS - A. Photographer - Period 1/04/95 - 31/03/96

Date	Detail	Chq	Total	VAT	Agents Comm.	Film & Process	Couriers	EquipHire Loc Exp	Props & Setbuild	Studio Costs	Assts Styl & Models	Motor Exp	Travel UK (Exp)	Overseas Trav/Loc	Teleph. & fax	Print, Post & Statnry	Subs & Pubs	Advert & Publty	Insurance	BkKeep & Accnty	Bank Chg & Interest	Repairs & Renewals	Drawings	Sundries
	Total by month		0.00	0.00	0.00	0.00	0.00	0.00	0.00	0.00	0.00	0.00	0.00	0.00	0.00	0.00	0.00	0.00	0.00	0.00	0.00	0.00	0.00	0.00
	Totals Year to Date		0.00	0.00	0.00	0.00	0.00	0.00	0.00	0.00	0.00	0.00	0.00	0.00	0.00									

Key to Abbreviations

Agents Comm.	Agent's Commission
Film & Process	Film & Processing
Couriers	Couriers
EquipHire Loc Exp	Equipment Hire & Location Expenses
Props & Setbuild	Props & Set Building
Studio Costs	Studio Costs
Assts Styl & Models	Assistants, Stylists & Models
Motor Exp	Motor Expenses
Travel UK (Exp)	Travel (UK) Expenses
Overseas Trav/Loc	Overseas Travel and Location Costs
Teleph. & fax	Telephone & Fax
Print, Post & Statnry	Printing, Postage and Stationery
Subs & Pubs	Subscriptions & Publications
Advert & Publty	Advertising & Publicity
Insurance	Insurance
BkKeep & Accnty	Bookkeeping & Accountancy
Bank Chg & Interest	Bank Charges & Interest
Repairs & Renewals	Repairs & Renewals
Drawings	Drawings
Sundries	Sundries

ILLUSTRATION 17

Petty Cash Expenditure - A. Photographer - Period 1/4/95 - 31/03/96

Date	Details	Total	VAT	Materials	Couriers	Motor Expenses	Travel Expenses	Subs & Pubs	Print, Post & Stationery	Drawings	Sundry
	Total by Month	0.00	0.00	0.00	0.00	0.00	0.00	0.00	0.00	0.00	0.00
	Total Year to Date	0.00	0.00	0.00	0.00	0.00	0.00	0.00	0.00	0.00	0.00

Invoice Listing - A. Photographer - Period 1/4/95 - 31/03/96							
Inv date	Client	Inv No	Net Value	VAT	Total	Unpaid value	Date paid
B/FWD	from previous year					0.00	
	Sub-total each month		0.00	0.00	0.00	0.00	
	Total Year to Date		0.00	0.00	0.00	0.00	

Permits

Royal Parks

In order to take pictures in the following Royal parks, governed by the Department of the Environment, you will need a permit:

St James Park	Abingdon Green (outside Palace of Westminster)
Green Park	Victoria Tower Gardens (outside Palace of Westminster)
Primrose Hill	Queen Victoria Memorial
Grosvenor Square	Hyde Park
Parliament Square	Kensington Gardens

How to Apply for a Permit

Central Royal Parks
To obtain a permit for the above Royal Parks, you must apply in writing on your own letterhead, to:

The Department of National Heritage
Events Office
Rangers Lodge
Hyde Park
London W2 2UH
Tel: 0171 - 298 2106

The following parks need to be applied for separately:

Richmond Park	*Greenwich Park*	*Bushey Park*	*Regents Park*
Holly Lodge	Charlton Way	Stock Yard	Store Yard
Richmond	Greenwich	Hampton Court Road	Inner Circle
Surrey	London	Hampton Hill	London NW1 4NR
TW10 5HS	SE10 8QY	Middlesex TW12 2EJ	

Hampstead Heath
The park has two areas governed by different park managers on separate numbers, which are:

Parliament Hill Fields (West Heath, Sandy Heath side)
Contact: Chris Murphy 0171 485 4491
Golders Hill
Contact: Peter Rouse 0181 455 5183

Battersea Park
Contact Tom Ridgway or Sue Valseca on 0181 871 7530/8800

In The City
It is advisable to ring the police station nearest to your location and inform them of your presence. Each shoot is assessed individually. Commercial fees are applied and indemnity forms have to be signed.

National Trust
Commercial photographers can photograph National Trust landscape and coastline free of charge, with the exception of major product advertising. For commercial photography of gardens and architectural exteriors and interiors, permission is required. To photograph National Trust properties, contact the National Trust Photographic Library who will put you in touch with the relevant Regional Office. All requests and location fees are assessed individually on their merit. Contact:

Maggie Gowan or Robert Morris
National Trust Photographic Library
36 Queen Anne's Gate
London SW1H 9AS
Tel: 0171 222 9251
Fax: 0171 447 6767

Useful Addresses

Advertising Standards Authority
2 Torrington Place
London WC1E 7HW
Tel 020 7580 5555
Fax 020 7631 3051

The Arts Council
14 Great Peter Street
London SW1P 3NQ
Tel 020 7333 0100
Fax 020 7973 6590

The Association of British Factors and Associates
1 Northumberland Avenue
Trafalgar Square
London WC2N 5BW
Tel 020 7930 9112

The Association of Photographers
81 Leonard Street
London EC2A 4QS
Tel 020 7739 6669
Fax 020 7739 8707

The British Association of Picture Libraries and Agencies (BAPLA)
18 Vine Hill
London EC1R 5DX
Tel 020 7713 1780
Fax 020 7713 1211

The British Photographers' Liaison Committee (BPLC)
c/o 81 Leonard Street
London EC2A 4QS
Tel 020 7739 6669
Fax 020 7739 8707

Business Technology Education Council (BTEC)
Central House
Upper Woburn Place
London WC1H 0HH
Tel 020 7413 8400
Fax 020 7387 6068

Chamber of Commerce
ATA Carnets
33 Queen Street
London EC4R 1AP
Tel 020 7248 4444
Fax 020 7489 0391
(EC Carnets no longer necessary)

Contributions Agency
DSS
Newcastle Upon Tyne NE98 1YX
Self Employed NI Contributions Enquiries
freephone 0800 393539
Local offices are listed according to postcode in the telephone book under 'Social Security' or 'Contributions Agency'

Copyright Licensing Agency
90 Tottenham Court Road
London W1P 0LP
Tel 020 7436 5931
Fax 020 7436 3986

The Design & Artists Copyright Society (DACS)
Parchment House
13 Northburgh Street
London EC1V 0AH
Tel 020 7336 8811
Fax 020 7336 8822

Education Recording Agency
Isis House
74 New Oxford Street
London WC1A 1EF
Tel 020 7436 4883
Fax 020 7636 2402

HM Customs & Excise
(for VAT registration)
PO Box 40
Carnborne Way
Damolly
Newry
Co. Down BT35 6PJ
Tel 0345 112114

HMSO (Crown Copyright)
St Crispins
Duke Street
Norwich
Norfolk NR3 1PD
Tel 0603 622211
Fax 0603 695583

Inland Revenue
local offices are listed according to postcode in the telephone book under 'Inland Revenue'

National Union of Journalists
Acorn House
314 Gray's Inn Road
London WC1X 8DP
Tel 020 7278 7916
Fax 020 7278 1812

Useful Forms, Pamphlets & Publications

FORMS

- Assisting Photographer's Invoice Forms - duplicate pad available from The Association of Photographers
- Delivery Note - duplicate pad available from The Association of Photographers, The British Association of Picture Libraries and Agencies or the National Union of Journalists
- Model Release Form - duplicate pad available from The Association of Photographers

PAMPHLETS

Inland Revenue

- CWL1 Starting in Business

Contributions Agency

- CWL1 Starting in Business
- CAL2 Guide to Tax for the Small Business
- CAL3 National Insurance Contrubtions Class 2 & 3
- CAO4 Paying by Direct Debit

Customs & Excise

- Should I be Registered for VAT?

Social Security

- ISO 20 - A Guide to Income Support, available from all Social Security Offices (Freeline Social Security Tel. 0800 666555)

PUBLICATIONS

- The ABC of UK Photographic Copyright, published by The British Photographers' Liaison Committee (see oposite) ISBN 0 9514671 1 5
- Artists' Handbooks, published by AN Publications, Tel 0191 567 3589
- Copyright Designs and Patents Act 1988, Chapter 48, published by HMSO (see opposite) ISBN 0 10 544888 5
- Super Highway Robbery - Freelances and the fight for copyright - by Lee Corner, published by the National Union of Journalists ISBN 0951457853

Index

Agents 47, 60, *(121)*
Art Orders 16, 34, 49
- Licence to Use 52, *(109)*
- Moral Rights Waiver 50
- Retrospective 52

Assisting Photographers 38
- Bookings 38-39
- Cancellation & Postponement 39
- Fees and Payment 39
- Invoicing 39, 62, *(111)*
- On location 39
- Passing off 44
- Public & Employer's Liability 80

Authorship 12, 13
Base Usage Rate 34, 52-53, *(117-120)*
Bookkeeping 62, 88, *(139-145)*
Bookings 34, 38
- Provisional 34
- Provisional (Assistants) 38

Borrowing Money (see 'Money')
Business Accounting 62-65, 87-91
- Business Plans 90
- Capital Expenditure 63
- Credit Control 88-89
- Depreciation/Capital Allowances 65
- Factoring 90
- Leasing 90
- Revenue Expenditure 64
- Trading - Sole Trader, Partnership or Limited Company 87
- See also: 'Invoicing', 'Money', 'National Insurance Contributions', 'Tax and Value Added Tax'

British Copyright Council (BCC) 57
Cancellation & Postponement 35, 39
Carnets 35, 148
Claiming Benefit 95-96
Collage 23
- Electronic Imaging 98, 102

Collecting Societies 18, 83-85
Common Law 11
Confidentiality 43
- Terms & Conditions 51

Contracts 49-55
- Licence to Use 52
- Moral Rights 28
- Third Parties 50-51
- Validity of Verbal Contract 49
- With client 45, 49-50
- With supplier 45, 89

Copyright Act 1911 & 1956 11
- Authorship 12
- Duration of 15

Copyright Designs & Patents Act 1988 11
- Authorship 12
- Duration of 14-15

Copyright 11-25
- Assignment of 13, 16, 17, 50, 73
- Assignment - Partial 13
- Authorship Joint 13
- Courts 24
- Electronic Imaging 99, 102-103
- Employed photographers 14, 27
- Europe 59
- in other people's work 23, 51
- Fair Dealing 21-22
- Infringement of Protected works 12, 23
- Residency Photographers 14
- Infringement and Legal Recourse 24
- Permitted Use 21-22
- 'Photograph', Definition of 12
- Students' Copyright 20
- Students - Experimentation 20
- Students - 'Criticism & Review' 21
- Students - 'Research & Private Study' 21

Criticism & Review 21
Customs & Excise 71, *(101, 103)*
Defamation 42
Delivery Notes 16, 33, 38, *(113)*, 149
Derogatory Treatment
- in Electronic Imaging 102
- Integrity Right 28
- Loss of Control 17
- Moral Right 30

Design & Artists' Copyright Society (DACS) 18, 85, 148
Digital & Electronic Imaging 97-103
- Collage 102-103
- Copyright 98-99
- Identification of the author 101
- Licensing 54, 100-101
- Moral Rights 101-102

Droit d'auteur 11, 31
Employer's Liability (see 'Liability')
Employment Schedule E 61
Estimates 18, 36, 49, *(105)*
Europe 57-60
- European Union 14, 57
- Copyright 59
- Pyramide 58
- Working abroad 60

Fair Dealing 21-22
False Attribution Right 28
Fees 33
- Pre-Production/Experimental & Speculative Photography 33

Goods In Trust 78
- Portfolios 33
- Props 46, 78

Harmonisation 57
- Professional Organisations 57
- Qualifications 59

Identification of an Author 16, 27
- in Electronic Imaging 101

Incidental Inclusion 22
Indemnity 51
- Insurance 80

Inland Revenue 61-62, *(125, 127, 129)*
- P45 form 62, *(125)*
- Tax Relief 63

Insurance 75
- Critical Illness 76
- Employer's Liability (see 'Liability')
- Equipment 77
- Film 35, 36, 45-46, 77
- Income Protection 75-76
- Loss of Business 76
- Motor 76
- Personal Accident 75
- Policy Excess 78-79
- Portfolio 33, 77
- Professional Indemnity 80
- Props 35, 78
- Public Liability (see 'Liability')
- Weather Contingency 35, 76-77
- Working abroad 81

Integrity Right 28
Intellectual Property 11
Internet 54, 103

Investments (see 'Money')
Invoicing 37, *(107)*
Advances 34
Expenses 34-35
Film & Processing Charges 34
Freelance Assistants 38, 39, *(111)*, 149
Model Fees 34
Non-payment 24, 89
Pre-Production Costs 33
Reshoot Expenses 36
Studio & Equipment Costs 35
Subcontractor Costs 35
Transport & Travel Costs 35
VAT 71, 72, 73
Liability 36
Business Trading 87
Employer's 35, 36, 79, 81
Public 36, 79, 81
Assistants 80
Third Party 50-51, 81
Licence to Use 13, 16-17, 37, 73, *(109)*
Advertising 19, 51, 52-53
All Uses 53
Art Orders 49-50
Digital Imaging 100-101
Editorial 53-54
Exclusive 18
Syndication 53-54
Model Fees 34
Child 34
Model Release Forms 37-38, 42, *(115)*, 149
Money
Borrowing 89
Commercial Lending 94
Financial Advice 94
Income Replacement 93
Pensions 91
Residential Mortgages 95
Savings & Investments 92
Moral Rights 27-31
Assertion of 16
Breach 30
Consent & Waiver of 29-30
Contracts 28
Duration of 29
Electronic Imaging 101-102
Employees 27
Europe 57-58
Exceptions 27
Transferability of 27
Waiver of 27, 29-30, 46
National Insurance Contributions 65-67
Class 1 and Schedule D 66
Class 2 and Exception 67, *(131)*
Class 4 and deferment 67-68, *(129)*
Contributions Agency DSS 65-68, *(127)*
NI Number 66
P60 form 62
Ownership of Film 13, 34, 51
Pamphlets & Publications 149
Passing Off 44
Photographic Assistants 44
Paternity Right 27-28, 30
Permits Royal Parks and National Trust 42-43, 147
Personal Accident Insurance (PAI) 75
Photomontage (see 'Collage')
Picture Libraries 20, 46-47, *(123)*
British Association of Picture Libraries & Agencies (BAPLA) 20, 46, 148, *(123)*
Pitching 33
Plagiarism 45
Portfolios **33**
Goods in Trust insurance 33
Insurance 77
Presentation of 33
Professional Organisations 148
Privacy 41-42
General Public 41
Model Release Forms 42
Personalities 41
Possible Legislation 42
Private & Domestic Commissions 29
Privacy Right 27
Professional Registration 60
Publisher's Right 23-24
Public Liability (see 'Liability')
Pyramide 58
Rejection of Work 36
Reproduction Rights 12
Research & Private Study 21
Revenue Expenditure 64
Secondary Rights 18, 84
Self-Employment 61-69
NI Contributions 67-68
Schedule D 61-62
Schedule D and Class 1 NI 66
'Speculative' Photography 33
Suppliers
Openings Accounts 89
Duty of Care 45-46
Contracts with 45, 89
Syndication 19
Art Orders 50
Licence to Use 53
Tax 61-69
Tax Year 62
Prizes & Awards 90
Self Assessment 68
Simple Tax Accounting 63
Terms & Conditions 18, 51-52, *(106, 108, 110)*
Third Part Indemnities 50-51
Trading Abroad 57-60
VAT 73
Trespass 42
Universal Declaration of Human Rights 11, 27
Value Added Tax 71-74
Cash Accounting 73
Invoicing 72
Registration 72-73, *(133)*
Returns 71, 73, *(137)*
Threshold 73
Trading abroad 73
Weather Insurance 35, 76-77